HOW FAR
I CAN GO

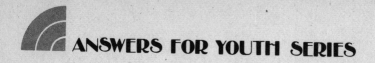

ANSWERS FOR YOUTH SERIES

HOW FAR I CAN GO

LARRY RICHARDS

Illustrations by Charles Shaw

ZONDERVAN
PUBLISHING HOUSE
OF THE ZONDERVAN CORPORATION
GRAND RAPIDS, MICHIGAN 49506

How Far I Can Go
Copyright © 1979 by the Zondervan Corporation
First published in 1968 by Moody Press, Chicago, under the title *How Far Can I Go?* Copyright ©1968 by Moody Bible Institute.

Zondervan Revised Edition 1979

Fifth printing August 1981

Library of Congress Cataloging in Publication Data

Richards, Lawrence O.
How far I can go.

(Answers for youth)
First published in 1968 under title: How far can I go?
SUMMARY: A discussion of dating and sex based on Scriptural values.
1. Sexual ethics. 2. Dating (Social customs) 3. Youth—Sexual behavior.
[1. Sexual ethics. 2. Dating (Social customs) 3. Conduct of life. 4. Christian life]
I. Title.

HQ32.R5   1979   301.41′42   79-15341
ISBN 0-310-38951-8

Unless otherwise indicated, Scripture quotations are taken from *The Living Bible,* © 1971 by Tyndale House Publishers, Wheaton, Illinois.

Printed in the United States of America

Contents

1

Under twenty-one

"Oh man," moaned Carl. "Here we go again." Ken leaned over his shoulder and nodded agreement. There it was, on the poster announcing that night's topic for youth group: "Avoiding Dating Dangers."

Carl struck an exaggerated pose with his feet apart and his finger shaking at the crowd of kids who began to gather.

"Now you young people," he began, picking up one of the sponsor's favorite phrases, "don't realize the explosive nature of se— er, of boy-girl relationships. Tonight we'll look at some of the pitfalls you can, er, fall into if you aren't careful. And to start off, let me tell you how it was when *I* was your age.

"First," Carl went on, shushing the little burst of laughter and groans that met his last remark, "in my day we avoided trouble by never being alone with a person of the opposite se— er, that we liked. We only saw each other when the whole group was around. We did things together. So, rule one is Don't date just one person. Date a crowd.

"Second, in my day we avoided trouble by going out only once a month. The rest of the time we studied. Things can't get too, er, friendly that way. After you've been dating a girl a year, you're still strangers! So, rule two is Don't date!

"Third, in my day we avoided trouble by dating around. We *never* went steady, even when we were engaged. One of the reasons for so much, er, trouble these days is that you young people go steady. So, rule three is Don't get involved with any one person. You might learn to like him."

"But Mr. Barnes," interrupted Judy, going along with Carl's act. "What kind of trouble could you possibly be talking about?"

"Say," chimed in Jack, "is it wrong to shake hands with your girl friend on the fifth date?"

"Well, hm— Er—" mumbled Carl, trying to look flustered. "When I was your age—"

"Hey, there you all are!" It was the real Bob Barnes, sticking his head around the corridor corner. "I've been looking for you. It's almost time to get started!"

Step into today's world of under twenty-one, and it comes through loud and clear. This isn't a world where rules from the dark ages offer much help. This isn't a world where the potencies and problems of sex can be avoided by pretending that s-e-x doesn't exist. It does exist. And Christian young people want to know how sex fits into their lives, now.

What kind of questions do the kids in high school and college have? That's what this book is all about. It's about what's really going on inside of Christian kids as they tussle with a force that plays a big role in your life. I hope this will be a frank book. An honest one. One that doesn't avoid the tough questions, or give pat answers. One that tries to help you think through the issues as a Christian.

So—let's jump in. What *are* the problems? What questions do Christian youth[1] have?

A dash of ignorance

That's how it all begins for most young teenagers struggling toward sexual maturity. A dash of ignorance, stirred well with confusion.

A nineteen-year-old Connecticut girl, looking back on her experience, says:

> Please try to relieve the fears of many, many girls about sex. Having been brought up in a "mum's the word about sex" home, I remember going home and crying after my first kiss (it was nothing passionate) thinking I had sinned terribly. There are so many other things that we have reason to feel guilty about—stealing, cheating, lying—but somehow sex has become a dominant fear in many girls' lives.

Such early fears may linger on. A girl of twenty asks,

> How do you find out about sex if your parents have told you very little? I get scared when I think of the responsibilities of being a wife. I've even been accused of being "afraid to love" because I wouldn't kiss a fellow I'd been dating one and a half years. And I guess I am.

Sex and relationships. These two go together. As a person moves through the teens into the twenties, he establishes and builds relationships. Girls build relationships with guys, guys with girls. And somehow, no one thinks or feels about *all* members of the opposite sex "like a brother" or believes that they're "just people."

An Illinois high school junior puts it this way: "Everyone is beginning to mature at this time and knows sex exists. The question is whether or not to experiment. The answer is always, 'Let's try it.' That's where kids

always get into trouble." "Always" seems like a pretty strong word. But experimentation seems characteristic of the dating life of many kids. Take Gene, an eighteen-year-old from a Minnesota suburb, now at a Christian college:

> I've gone with a girl for two and a half years. During that time we've done some things that are not considered "right." What I wonder is this: what's OK and what's wrong? I've heard lots of answers and they don't all agree. It's bothering me so much that I can't even kiss her good night anymore without thinking about this type of thing. What can I do? Help!

Gene adds:

> I've talked with a bunch of my friends here at school and

we found out that this problem is common to all of us. I
didn't know this when I first started writing, so I guess
they must be universal—Christian and non-Christian.

Why do kids get in this spot? There seem to be lots of
reasons.

A California eighteen-year-old analyzes:

> Sex problems in high school arise in basically what's
> proper action on a date. Going to drive-ins with your date,
> three hours in the dark separated by just a few feet, and
> usually not separated, but with your arm around the girl,
> well, to say the least, the movie is not going to get undi-
> vided attention. Where's the line? Kissing? Where do you
> quit? What do you expect of the second date, third, etc?

A Michigan teen agrees.

> The problem teens face with sex is the "evolution of the
> date." By the third date if not sooner the couple begins to
> neck. I think maybe a slim majority don't go any further
> than this most of the time. The reason making out appeals
> to teens is that it excites our emotions. Making out also
> gives the date the feeling that he really likes the person. I
> have a friend who told me that he would like to go "all the
> way" with his girl because it seemed *so* right and the
> natural thing to do.

The natural thing to do

That's only part of the problem. Sure, sexual desires
and expression of affection are natural. But other things
complicate them. A big factor today is pressure from the
peer group. A Pennsylvania fellow sees that this way:

> The main problem high schoolers have in the area of sex
> is the social pressure of the group. Many high schoolers
> are confused by the standards of their friends. They are
> searching for guidelines because the world around them
> shows nothing but the importance of sex if you want to be
> somebody or a part of the group.

An Illinois girl says:

> Sex is "the thing to do" in high school. Some kids are looked down on if they are not involved in this area, and consequently they feel out of it. Girls will become involved in sex for the popularity aspect.

Linda, a senior, sees the average girl's problem clearly:

> Often high school girls who don't date or date very little tend to relax their standards in hopes of attracting guys. They think that by "giving a little" they will get more dates and have a happier social life. It's a strong temptation to lower standards in order to be able to have fun like the rest of the kids.

"Just experimenting" has a strong attraction too. "I feel," says a sixteen-year-old girl, "that to many of us sex is something to experiment with—something that can identify us with the adult world."

"Just experimenting" often awakes what Judy, a Michigan girl, labels "just plain lust." She says:

> Even as a Christian I've had some very trying times with just plain lust. I never really knew how strong—how very, very forceful—the attraction physically was between a guy and a gal who think themselves in love. It's so *easy* to go wrong.
>
> Guys I guess, prove their masculinity to themselves, to the girls, and to the other guys by fulfilling the sex act. Girls feel loved and needed—such a coveted feeling—for a while. Sex is so important today. We learn very young how to twist our legs, how to sit rather "sexily," how to apply "mysterious" makeup. TV teaches us how to kiss and twist our figures the right way.
>
> Sex has just become the focal point around which everything revolves. Sex, sex, sex! It becomes so impressed on our minds that we never realize it or desire to change.

Another dimension

Sex for the sake of sex is a real problem for many these days. But there's another important dimension. Many kids don't get involved for lust's sake. Their problem sneaks up on them because of love.

An Indiana girl puts it this way:

> High schoolers are not all too young to really feel love. When two people are genuinely affectionate toward each other their physical relations usually grow at the same pace as their feelings for each other.

A Colorado girl comes out strongly in favor of such involvement. She asks,

> Why not have sex? Many kids find the guy they are going to marry in high school. Why not express your love for him? If you both have an agreement not to go all the way, why not?

This issue is a big one for lots of older youth. If sex plays such a big role in marriage, why shouldn't some sexual involvement be a natural part of any love relationship?

A California girl asks,

> How are you supposed to show affection for a guy that you're not necessarily in love with, and yet you like *a lot?* I don't think you have to be engaged to let him kiss you good night, but on the other hand, how far is too far? It's terribly unrealistic to say that a couple is going together for six months, and end up with a light peck on the cheek.

Karen, an Illinois sophomore, shares her thoughts:

> High school kids have a problem of knowing just what they can do and still be decent and self-respecting persons. We go home and hint to our parents because we want some information, not because we have dirty minds, but because we simply don't know what's going on. It's

hard to live a teen's life when we do not even know what
is expected of us. I can't figure out what is normal.

What is right? What's normal? How do we build good
relationships with the opposite sex? "How far" is right on
a casual date? Between steadies? For engaged couples?
And, most of all, *why?*

There are lots of answers suggested in today's world.
But it's important to find the *right* answers. Why? Partly
because sex isn't an isolated function in a person's life. It's
something that's related to the very heart of our personalities and our feelings about ourselves. And sex, out
of perspective and out of control, can warp us as persons
and warp our lives.

When you put it all together, it's a complex problem.
Christian kids know the Bible makes some pretty flat
statements about sex. "Sexual sin," it says in 1 Corinthians 6:13, "is never right: our bodies were not made for
that, but for the Lord, and the Lord wants to fill our
bodies with Himself." But, a lot of kids honestly wonder,
what constitutes sexual sin? Is it just intercourse, just
going all the way?

So, what about it? What is right? What's wrong? How
far should we go? There are lots of suggestions floating
around today. We'll look at some common ones in the
next three chapters. The Bible has some important things
to say too. We'll look at these in chapters 5 and 6. And in
the last few chapters we'll try to put it all together.

We may not come up with "precise rules." But we'll
sure try hard to discover how to "use every part of your
body to give glory back to God, because He owns it" (1
Cor. 6:20). And that "every part" means glory in the
rightful enjoyment of His gift of sexuality, as well as glory
in a conscience that's pure and free to find the best in
relationships with the opposite sex now.

Steps to take

Before you read on, take a minute or two to jot down your thoughts on the following issues. Just a little time out between chapters can make reading this book a far more helpful experience.

1. What is your attitude toward sex? Write down what you think and feel about it.

2. Do any of the quotes in this first chapter express your feelings or experiences? Jot down questions you'd particularly like answered as you read on.

2

Everybody's doing it

A look around high schools and colleges seems to confirm the idea. Ann, an Iowa junior, sees it this way:

Within the past year one of the most brilliant girls in my class has become pregnant, gone to Mexico for her baby, and returned to resume schooling. Another girl who is a cheer leader, in National Honor Society, and wealthy, is going steady and has been for several years. Her boyfriend says the only reason he goes with her is because he can get her to go all the way whenever he wants. Just last week another girl returned after having had her baby. This girl had been engaged, and was going to move to California as soon as she got married after her junior year in high school. She never got married, but the father, quite handily, left for the service.

The newspapers seem to confirm Ann's impression that most of the kids go all the way with sex. Take this report in a Chicago newspaper:

At least 200,000 unmarried girls of high school age in the nation had abortions last year, a third of all brides under 18 were pregnant when married, and the mothers of

20 percent of the illegitimate children born were under 17, according to Dr. William M. Goins, director of a maternity and infant-care project in a Detroit hospital.

Stop and realize that many teen couples never get "caught," that many more who don't go all the way are still involved in heavy petting; and you get the idea that sex play is the normal thing for high school and college youth. It really does seem that everyone is doing it.

Why?

Why is everybody doing it? There is a variety of reasons, but one seems to be that *everyone thinks everyone else is doing it too!*

"Kids are afraid nowadays," says a sophomore girl, "that if they don't neck or pet when they're out on a date the guys won't like them and won't go out with them again. Christians are the same way even though they shouldn't be. Also it's the 'in' thing to do and if you don't follow the crowd you're out of it."

A seventeen-year-old fellow from Pennsylvania agrees:

> I believe that many kids engage in illicit sexual relations for the social prestige. Obviously, this is not the only motive, but a good number of kids will do things because of the group that they normally wouldn't even consider doing.

It's terribly important for most kids to feel that they belong. Even kids who have everything going for them. Bob, a strapping blond football player friend of mine who's at a Christian college, tells how he felt trying to gain acceptance in a high status group in his high school:

> I found as a junior and senior particularly a big problem in wanting to be in the popular group composed of athletes and good-looking girls. I continually kept contact

with this one particular group and tried to associate with them. I found in my junior year I didn't have much success in my attempt to be a part. But in my senior year I was able to really belong and to become a part because of my athletic success.

However, I was in a state of confusion because I realized that, in order to be a part of this group, it was necessary for me to be a part of their activities and support their standards. As a Christian I knew that I could not or should not succumb to their standards. This caused a great deal of emotional strain. I knew what a Christian would do, but how could I do this and keep my status with the group?

The dilemma was particularly bad because of my relationship with one particular girl. She was very attractive and had a lot of status in the group. She dated one of the other guys up until football season my senior year. Then she switched attention to me, primarily because I was in the limelight socially. (At the time I felt it was due to true feeling and admiration for me as a person.) I told her some of my feelings about Christianity, and how torn I was between my peer group and Christ.

Then I decided to put my Christian convictions into action. I continued to go to the parties, but I wouldn't participate in any of the drinking, smoking, etc. I just tried to have fun with the kids and be as nonchalant about the whole affair as possible. My girl friend had different ideas. She wasn't ready to give up her good times. I thought many times of chucking the whole idea and just trying to hold on, because I thought after a while the kids would accept me as I wanted to be rather than according to their standards. However, it didn't work out that way. The girl started dating other guys, and would discuss with them my changes and intentions. Before I knew it, I felt very uncomfortable with this group, and it wasn't too long before I was out of it completely.

It really hurts to be out of it. But everyone, like Bob, knows that to be "in" you've got to "be a part of their activities and support their standards."

What does this mean for sex? If *everybody's* doing it, the

Christian kid may feel he has to too, to be "in" *anywhere!*

It seems especially tough on the girls. "It's a strong temptation for the girls," writes an eighteen-year-old in an East Coast Bible college, "to lower standards in order to be able to have fun like the rest of the kids. I think this same thing can carry through into college, with even worse consequences."

Is everybody doing it?

"Many high schoolers wonder," writes Carol, a senior from Pennsylvania, "whether in ten years *all* girls when they are married will have had sexual intercourse. I do."

When you're convinced that everybody's doing it, you

wonder if you're the only oddball! That's what bothered a girl in a secular college who commented desperately, "I'm still a virgin, but I don't know how long I can hold out. Everybody's doing it." Yet a survey of her dorm showed *that ninety percent of the girls there were virgins too!*

The Sex Information and Education Council of the United States states in a study of premarital sexual standards that "the common belief that the proportion of non-virginity has risen markedly during the past twenty years is not supported by the evidence of research."[1]

To check this out, one of my students did a study at an Illinois high school. Some of the reactions to questions about moral values and sexual activity are pretty surprising to the fellow or girl who thinks that everybody is doing it. The results may be even more surprising to evangelical kids, who have the idea at times that *at least* all nonChristian kids are doing it. Here are some typical responses from teens who don't attend evangelical churches:

"I think sex relations are for married couples *only*. If a boy doesn't respect your judgment then he doesn't think much of you as a person." The same girl goes on: "I kiss (I guess you can say neck) but it never gets very much farther than that. He says I'm an iceberg and it makes me feel sort of good, 'cause I know it's true. He respects my morals, so that makes a lot of things a lot easier."

A Protestant girl who bases her morals "on my mood" still says, "I am definitely not a plaything and will not be taken advantage of."

A Catholic girl says her morals are "to save my body for the man I marry and to keep my reputation and soul clean. Maybe you might lose some dates for not giving in, but those guys you lose aren't worth it. On the long run you find it pays off."

A girl who goes to no church puts it very strongly:

> I definitely believe that a girl should be a virgin when
> she gets married. A girl with morals does not engage in
> petting, intercourse, etc. I think a couple loves and under-
> stands each other more when there is no type of petting,
> etc., going on.

How do we get the impression that everybody's doing
it if there are kids around who have such definite
standards?

For one thing, there *are* more people involved in premarital sex. Say you're in a high school of two hundred,
and in two years four girls become pregnant. Then you
move to a high school of a thousand. If the percentage
stays the same, you'll hear of twenty girls becoming pregnant each year! In the small school the news breaks only
once a semester or so, and soon is submerged in campus
activities. But in the larger school a new case crops up
every other week! No wonder it seems everybody's doing
it!

Another thing is that today we're much more willing to
talk about sexual matters. And many kids who really
think it isn't wrong to have intercourse (but aren't doing
it) are quick to say so. The attitudes toward premarital sex
are changing a lot faster than the behavior.

Whatever the reason for the impression we sometimes
get, the facts show that everybody *doesn't*. All rumor to
the contrary, most don't go all the way.

While this doesn't necessarily say anything about petting, it does make it pretty clear that the line "Everybody
does it" is just that: a line. A wrong-headed idea guys get
that may lead them to believe their dates expect to be
handled. And a wrong-headed idea girls get that makes
them feel "abnormal" if they resist.

A price to pay

Even if sex isn't something that everybody does, we often feel that it's a price we have to pay for acceptance. "Do you have to make out every time you date a boy?" asks a seventeen-year-old Iowan. Another girl puts the question even straighter: "Is sex the way to show appreciation?"

"I do feel," says a college boy, "that one of the biggest problems high schoolers have is establishing a relationship with someone of the opposite sex. They are afraid they will be 'put down' and are afraid of failure."

Often kids who are unsure of themselves resort to sex play as the safest way to avoid failure. It's surely true that invitations to date come fast and heavy when a girl doesn't hold out. But everybody knows why.

"A friend of mine heard of something a friend of his did with a particular girl. He tried to date this girl with the intent to do the same things with her." The word gets around, and suddenly you get "popular." Not because of who you are and your personality or because you're fun to be with and the guys like *you*, but just because you're an available laboratory for a guy who wants to experiment with sex!

That's a pretty high price for popularity—to stop being thought of and valued as a person, and be asked out just because you let yourself be used.

There are guys and girls to date who will be interested in you for yourself. They may not be easy to find, and waiting may hurt. But it's a lot easier than paying the price of lowered standards for dates or for popularity.

How do you locate the guys and girls who feel like you do? A while ago we heard from kids (not even evangelical kids) with high standards. Think it's funny you don't hear from them in school? Or that the talk and gossip centers on the kids who *do*, not the ones who *won't?* Aside from the obvious (after all, which is more exciting to talk about!), the fact is that lots of times kids with the stricter standards don't speak up. When a guy says straight out that sex is fun, and that all the rules against it are just a plot of society and of parents who don't want to pay the bills, who wants to stick his neck out and disagree? So you get the impression that everybody agrees with him. Silence gives assent. But the chances are that lots of the kids listening to him *don't agree.* Like you, they're just waiting for someone else to speak out.

There's a lot of evidence that the peer group can push kids into doing things they believe aren't right. But some experiments on conformity to group pressure have shown that *the presence of a single dissenter* can be enough to break the spell and help those who don't want to follow the crowd.

Maybe, right now, there are kids on your campus or in your church feeling pressured because "everybody does it" who wouldn't pay the price if they knew *you* don't. Or maybe you can look back and wish someone had had guts enough to speak up before you paid a price that's cost you more than you dreamed it could.

Today we need stable standards to "see clearly the difference between right and wrong, and to be inwardly clean" (Phil. 1:10). To the Christian such standards are the outgrowth of a free response to a God who loves us and whom we love. "Don't act thoughtlessly," says the Bible, "but try to find out and do whatever the Lord wants you to" (Eph. 5:17).

Stable standards don't come from "yourself alone." They don't come from the trends of the day. They come when *you* honestly try to find out and to *do* what the Lord wants you to do. Live this way, and you'll be "a new and different person with a fresh newness in all you do and think. Then you will see from your own experience how his ways will really satisfy you" (Rom. 12:2).

Steps to take

1. Do you think everybody's doing it on your campus? Jot down the names of kids whom you *know* have different standards from yours. Try making another list of kids who believe and behave as you do.

   Now, circle the names of your *friends* on each list.

   Finally, think a minute. What does the relative length of each list and the placement of the circles say to you? What do they say *about* you?

2. Look through the chapter again, and compare the suggested passages of Scripture. What does each Bible passage say?

   Ephesians 5:8-13
   Romans 5:3-5
   Ephesians 2:1-3
   3 John 11

3. Check back over the question list you made up after reading chapter 1. See answers to any of them yet?

3

Fun, fun, fun

"High schoolers," says a New Jersey fellow, "do not really consider sex a problem. Rather it's something to go after and to have fun with."

Lots of things help build this impression. The things the other kids say. The ideas we get from movies and magazines and advertising and books. But probably the biggest thing that fixes the idea is a little bit of experience. It's fun to hold hands. It's more fun to kiss your date. The closer you get, the more exciting and pleasurable it is.

A New York girl says:

> We've been brought up on the idea that sex as a general rule is forbidden. We realize that our parents love us, and that they don't want us in trouble, but it becomes more fascinating when you're with a guy, petting, etc. It seems all right and very enjoyable, but when you're apart, you feel guilty about it. But no matter how much you resolve not to do it again, it happens as soon as you get together. Lots of kids, including myself, have managed to keep from going all the way. But many more haven't.

Pleasurable. Fascinating. Enjoyable. No wonder in high school and college "sex is made to look not only desirable but right." How "right"? A college student from Pennsylvania describes it this way:

> Kids see sex everywhere encouraged and displayed on TV, at the movies, in the way their fathers and other adults look at other women, etc. Yet they are told it is all wrong, and is taboo. They feel either their parents are hypocrites, or just trying to prevent them from having a good time. They think that sex cannot be wrong because of the feeling of excitement, etc., that they get when they have some sex contact.

Another young man simply says, "Why not, if pleasurable?"

Lots of times ideas like these find their way into fellows' lines. Maybe you've heard (or used) some yourself! Lines that build on the idea that since sex is fun and exciting, that since it's so natural, that since it "seems so right," we ought to let ourselves go a little.

Maybe you want to buy the fun philosophy of sex. But before you do, here are some things you may want to think about.

The bunny buggy

You've seen it. The jaunty long-eared profile of *Playboy* magazine's sex symbol on the windows of guys' cars. Probably better than anything else it "says" what a lot of fellows feel about sex.

Note that I said guys. Some girls buy the *Playboy* idea too. But the basic appeal is to the guys.

Part of the reason is the way men are built—physically and emotionally. Their sex drive is closer to the surface, they're easier to arouse and they're more likely to seek sex as a biological act apart from love. To fellows the "fun" view of sex is really appealing.

Research has shown that there *are* pretty basic differences between the male and female attitude toward sex. Here are a couple of significant cases. A study of the motives of college students who had premarital intercourse showed that the guys' number one reason for going all the way was to gain physical pleasure. (Curiosity was second.) Only 5 percent gave "love" as their motive! On the other hand, girls overwhelmingly went "all the way" because they thought they were in love. Another interesting reaction comes from teens who believe it is OK to go all the way on a date. What are their reasons? For the girl it was, again, "I love him." But for the guy the big reason was *"I like it!"*

Now, there's nothing wrong about "liking" sex. In fact, God planned our bodies so that we *would* like it. But sometimes we're led to some peculiar conclusions from the fact that sex is, at its best, exciting and pleasurable for both sexes.

Playboy magazine presents its philosophy clearly. Sex with or without love "can be one of the most profound and rewarding elements in the adventure of living." Not only is sexual activity perfectly legitimate, but "chastity" is an unreasonable repression of a basic human need.

This argument too has strong appeal to the fellows. Unlike females, whose monthly cycle isn't keyed to sexual desire, a male's body is constantly at work making seminal fluid, a liquid designed to carry sperm when they're released. The sacs in which the seminal fluid is stored have a limited capacity. When they fill, there's a definite physical pressure inside that triggers a fellow's sexual desires and feelings. So a male's physical makeup includes a sex pressure buildup; a pressure that can set strong sex desire off with an overwhelming rush.

No wonder the idea that chastity is an "unnatural repression" appeals! Tag such repression not only unnatural but harmful, and the sex-is-fun philosophy sounds pretty reasonable. After all, it's not *moral* to harm anyone—even yourself. So why frustrate yourself when the solution is so natural and so enjoyable?

One problem with this view is that, no matter how plausible it may sound, the results aren't as beneficial as they're purported to be. Dr. Francis J. Braceland, clinical professor at Yale and editor of the *American Journal of Psychiatry*, reports that premarital sex relations have "greatly increased the number of young people in mental hospitals." More lenient attitudes toward sex "have imposed stresses on some college women severe enough to cause emotional breakdown."

Dr. J. Irvin Sands of the Neurological Institute of New York says:

> My own experience in dealing with many neurotic and psychotic people . . . has led me to conclude that premarital sexual activity by females leaves a blight on the emotional part of their personality. These activities are a source of emotional conflict.

You can see it in teens who've tried a taste of sex "fun" but are troubled afterwards. A seventeen-year-old Catholic girl writes, "I've engaged in light petting and once or twice in heavy petting. I always say I'm never going to do it again, but sometimes it just happens and I feel absolutely miserable." Even if it were just girls who are troubled by premarital sex, that should say something to guys who respect girls as *persons*, not simply as objects. If it isn't moral to harm yourself, it surely isn't moral to do something that may harm someone else. And premarital sex relations *can* harm!

Sick society

But if some people are emotionally troubled, isn't it because society has put such unnatural restrictions on premarital sex? In other societies premarital sex isn't always discouraged. In some it has even been *encouraged!*

The Palauans arranged for their young women to serve a year as prostitutes in a neighboring village. The Masai encouraged their young men to have mistresses, the only restrictions being that they were not to cause pregnancy. Dr. Nida tells of two tribes, the Korango and Mesakin of the Nuba Hills, who commented thus on their almost complete premarital sexual license: "We are like goats."[1] It's not *sex* that's wrong, the argument goes. It's the fact that society *regulates* sex that causes the trouble.

There are several problems though with this view. While there are cultures (like those mentioned above) where the sex practices are much freer than in our society, the fact is that "at no time or place and in no primitive stage of culture have men been able to live without *some* form of restraint" in the area of sex. "A state of primitive promiscuity, anthropologists now tell us, where sex life was simply spontaneous or was allowed to take its own natural course with no pattern at all imposed upon it by the group, never existed."[2] Somehow every society has had to regulate that "natural" sexual desire.

Now, some may say that sex is in a mess today because we regulate its expression. But why does *everyone* have to regulate it? It may very well be that the regulations aren't the cause of the problems we have with sex, but that the problems we have with sex are the cause of the regulations! We put speed limits on roads because it seems "natural" to some people to go so fast they endanger themselves and others. Yet who sees the speed laws as a *cause* of speeding?

It's important to understand this term "natural." For instance, let's say that you're angry (a strong emotion, as is aroused sexual desire). In the heat of the moment you attack another person with a gun or a knife or brick, or whatever is at hand. Would you go to court and base your defense on the argument that the attack was "natural" in view of the way you felt at the time?

Somehow, *naturalness* in this case doesn't seem adequate justification for the behavior.

That's what you're for

There's another more serious assumption that underlies the whole sex-is-fun philosophy. A fourteen-year-old freshman expressed it clearly when he wrote, "I don't feel sex is bad, because that's what you're for." He's saying, as is Hugh Hefner, that the Korango view of man is the accurate one: We are like goats.

To this teen, to Hefner, and to the Korango, man is basically a biological being. The physical is to be the controlling element in our lives, and the satisfaction of physical desires the highest good. This isn't a new attitude. In Jeremiah's day God called His people "well-fed lusty stallions, each neighing for his neighbor's wife," and added, "Shall I not punish them for these things? says the LORD; and shall I not avenge myself on a nation such as this?" (Jer. 5:7-9 RSV).

Lusty stallions? Goats? No, God created man in His image. There's something more than the biological inside—and our experience proves it.

Most of us know what nineteen-year-old Jim expresses: "Once involved, a person *wants* to get out but continually goes back. This, of course, is the boy's points of view. He wants the pleasure again, and each time he gains it, it gains more of a grip on him. How can he get away?"

Purely physical release doesn't bring relief. It may bring bondage. Jim discovered what Ralph Eckert, former head of the University of Connecticut's Department of Family Development, point out: "Unless sexual release is associated with a feeling of love, it may be only very *temporarily* tension-reducing. In the long run it may actually be sexually *stimulating*, with real satisfaction painfully absent."[3] Sex as a biological act brings release to goats and stallions. But to men and women who seek sex as sex, it proves terribly disappointing.

Sex for sex's sake (as that "natural" biological urge) does more than increase the hold of sexual desire. A California Christian teen says:

I was having a long relationship with one girl that was becoming pretty sexually loaded. After being away from her at college for about 3 months, in a knot of emotional conflict (mostly over sex), I resolved that this type of relationship was more detrimental to both of us than we imagined. Especially as it was taken so casually. I decided that before I lost all my self-respect and that which I had for the girl, I would deemphasize the sex and try to be a good friend instead of lover.

Casual sex doesn't bother goats. But it does not build respect between persons.

Casual sex is something fellows and girls often misunderstand about each other. A boy too easily believes the girl wants the pleasure of casual sex. And the girl too easily believes that the boy wants *her*. When a guy regularly uses a girl, she becomes just another accessory—like a car or a hi-fi or a TV set. She's entertainment, not as a person who's worthwhile and valued for herself, but as an object. Proof? Just ask the guys. While some girls say they might go all the way "if I loved the guy," the boys say, "I'd try—*if I didn't respect her!*"

What's to do?

One thing is, *recognize what we are*. While we're not *just* physical beings, the physical does play a big part in our experience. This is especially important to men. That "sex pressure buildup" is really there.

The pressure doesn't have to be released through intercourse though. A safety valve has been built into a man's physical makeup. It's called "nocturnal emission" or, more commonly, a "wet dream." When the seminal fluid fills up the sacs, it spills over at night during sleep, usually accompanied by a sex dream. This safety valve, not intercourse, is all a boy needs to "avoid endless frustration." That line "You'll frustrate me if you don't" and "If you really cared you wouldn't let me suffer this way" is, again, a line.

But don't forget: a man _is_ easily aroused, and his sexual desire easily triggered. "I know how guys react and what can trigger them into sexual desire," says Kay, a junior. "When I want to go out with a guy, I wear very modest clothes because I'm not about to turn someone else on. If he doesn't like my clothes, too bad." Kay has some other strong ideas too. She goes on:

> I'll never kiss a guy until I've been going with him at least six months. If he can wait that long, then he's interested in me as a person, not just a body. I'll never let anyone except my husband go further than just kissing. I hate it when guys look at me or any other girl with that look in their eyes. It's stupid. It makes us lose our respect. Honestly, a girl is _not_ just a piece of meat.

A second thing is _remember who we are_. Yes, we're physical beings. But we're far more than that.

This is true for Christians and non-Christians alike. Even after the fall, Genesis reminds us that "God created man in his own image" (Gen. 1:27 RSV). Even men who think of themselves as being "like goats" aren't. Even they have some concept that certain behavior is right to engage in, and other behavior is wrong. They may not know or accept God's standards but, as Dr. Nida points out, they do have _some_ standards. They regulate themselves and their society by principles other than immediate satisfaction of physical instinct.

Really, the idea Why not if pleasant? is awfully naïve. All of us have learned by the teens and twenties that immediate satisfaction of every desire is impossible and foolish. Sure, it's more pleasant to eat sundaes and shakes and candy than meals. If you want to be a fat slob. But who wants that? So we learn to limit our pleasures because we want some greater good.

When my children were preschoolers they loved to spend their nickels and dimes. Get a couple of cents, and it's off to the store. Someday they'll want something big. Maybe a bike, or if they're older, a motorcycle. And they'll learn that while it's fun to spend money as soon as you get it, the only way you can get the big items is to deny yourself the pleasure of spending *now*.

That's what the Apostle Paul was talking about when he wrote, "I keep my body under." Like an athlete in training, Paul determined to control his body, not to let his body control him.

Don't get the idea that Paul was a fanatic old ascetic, a little nuts on the idea of sexual abstinence. After all, it was Paul who labeled as a "doctrine of demons" the idea that everyone ought to abstain from marriage, and he reminds us that "everything created by God is good, and nothing is to be rejected if it is received with thanksgiving (1 Tim. 4:4 RSV). God created sex "to be received with thanksgiving by those who believe and know the truth" (v. 3). But Paul did warn about losing control.

So, we're back to our original problem. It's not a question of letting yourself have fun and being "natural." It's a question of *how* to regulate yourself—a question of what's wrong, what's right, and why. We *are* persons, made in God's image, and so given the freedom and responsibility of being more than animals. That means living responsibly and valuing each other as persons. We're free not to trivialize sex by using each other for physical thrills.

You *can* buy the bunny view that sex is purely physical, and exists for fun, fun, fun. But you'll be denying *who* you are as a person. And you'll be denying who you are as

a Christian. For whatever God wants you to do about sex,
He doesn't want you to downgrade yourself and
others—His highest creations—to the level of goats.

Steps to take

1. Look again at Kay's philosophy of dating life (p. 35).
    If you disagree in *any* way, try to spell out what
    you think would be a better approach.

2. Now look through the chapter again, and list
    carefully arguments you can think of *for* or *against*
    the viewpoint you outlined above.

3. For girls: The chapter mentions several lines fel-
    lows may use. Take a minute and jot down the
    answer you'd give to each of them.

4. Study these Scripture passages, and write down
    in your own words what they say:
    Ephesians 5:2-7
    Romans 2:12-16
    Ecclesiastes 2:1-11

4

But we're in love

A California girl writes:

When two people really fall in love, though they may be
in high school, they wonder about why they can't have
each other. Sure, they know "thou shalt not . . ." and all.
But they begin to wonder about their own personal feelings and the love and desire they feel for the other person.

As one girl asked, "Since you're getting to know the
one you love better intellectually and socially, why not
physically?"

These kids are all reflecting a common attitude these
days. The attitude that while sex without affection is less
than human and wrong, sex with love is pure and good
and right.

The Sex Information and Education Council guide on
premarital standards points out four major premarital sex
standards: abstinence; the double standard (boys can,
nice girls don't); permissiveness without affection (the
playboy approach); and permissiveness with affection.
"Permissiveness with affection," the guide says, "has

today achieved a respectability and sizeable minority following among both sexes."[1]

What is "permissiveness with affection"? It's the idea that "love" makes it right, with "love" meaning to most people a "subjective feeling of deep affection based upon detailed acquaintance with the other party." This isn't one of those rabbit-hutch relationships in which any guy or girl will do. It's a relationship in which each person really cares for the other as a person and finds the physical expression of that love an acceptable and valued thing.

The idea that love makes it right has a sizeable following in high school and college. As a college freshman from Maryland says, "While at least one social circle in almost every high school practices intercourse, *many* of the other kids believe premarital sex is OK, but only for that 'special guy someday.'"

A check into a nearby high school showed that she's right. While many kids come out squarely against premarital intercourse (as shown in chap. 2), many others disagree. "I don't believe in premarital sex for *me*," says seventeen-year-old Debbi. "Maybe for other couples who are really in love it's all right. I don't think anyone should have anything to say except the couple themselves." Debbi's idea that love is the big thing is also shown in her further comment on petting: "I have never gone all the way but I have come close. I never thought anything I did was wrong because I really thought at the time that I was in love."

The love motif is a big one where the girls are concerned. Karen, who also thought of love as justification, *now* looks back and sees absence of real love as the reason for dissatisfaction with her experiences:

> I have had *extensive* sexual activity with two boys. I feel

now this was more out of experimentation than love, but at the time I thought it *was* out of love. I now see that emotions are difficult to rule one, and for me, as an individual, a long time is needed to really discover my feelings. Now I want to date as many boys as possible, to see and explore each individual boy as a person before engaging in sexual activity.

Kids from evangelical churches have a similar problem understanding the role of the physical when two young people are in love. As an Illinois nineteen-year-old writes, "The *Christian* questions whether it's really wrong. The philosophy is very

prevalent that 'If I love him (her) why not go ahead?' This
is hard to fight."

Why fight it?

Should we dismiss the idea that physical expression of
love is all right? If it's important in marriage, why not in
dating? Doesn't love make it right?

Many writers and ethical thinkers attempt to work out a
morality based on a dynamic understanding of the role of
love in our lives. This ethical thinking draws on the Bible
and builds its arguments on the biblical concept of love.
"If you love your neighbor as much as you love yourself,"
the Bible says, "you will not want to harm or cheat him, or
kill him or steal from him." So, the passage goes on to say,
"Love does no wrong to anyone. That's why it fully
satisfies all of God's requirements" (Rom. 13:9-10).

If sex as something "natural" appeals to boys, sex as an
expression of love strikes a deeply responsive chord in a
girl's personality. Remember the reasons college kids give
for engaging in premarital intercourse? For the boys it
was the pleasure, but for girls it was "because I loved
him!"

It's the girls *in love,* not those who are just curious, who
are most likely to find sexual expression—from petting to
intercourse—acceptable and "right." While boys tend to
refrain from pressuring girls they respect into sex, girls
generally respond only to the fellows they really like!

Now, it's clear that the "I love you" approach to sex is a
lot better than the "I love *it*" approach. Motive *is* important. In or out of marriage, sex without love is something
less than fully human. But even if sex with affection is
better than some approaches that doesn't mean it's necessarily the best.

As a matter of fact, just a quick look around makes it

clear that as a guideline for teens and those in their twenties, "We love each other" has some pretty big loopholes.

A little honest reflection makes all of us admit that there have been times we thought we were in love but weren't. One study shows an average of five "real loves" for kids between the ninth grade and the second year of college. Each time it's easy to think, "This is it." But how do we know?

An Illinois senior says:

I just broke up with a girl who was, for a while, the greatest thing that walked. I thought I was in love with her and she with me, but we were wrong. I'm a senior and I'm too young to really know, but how will I know when the right girl comes? I think that is the big problem.

"Many kids in my class," says an Iowa graduate, "and others I have known have planned marriage and then called it off because at the last minute they discovered it wasn't really love, but just emotion."

If love can fool you right up to marriage, how can you be sure when you give yourself to "that special person" that he or she really *is* the one you'll marry?

"Kids in high school," says a California girl, "misinterpret their physical attraction to someone as love. They don't know how to distinguish between physical desires and true emotions toward a person."

Physical stimulation isn't the only hidden motive. "Many girls," says a fifteen-year-old, "think that the only way to keep a fellow is to have sex relations with him. I think many think they're in love when they're just fond, or just want the security of a date every Saturday."

Another girl agrees: "High school and college girls want a man around so they can be wanted by somebody."

Being wanted is so important to many girls. One study

of teenage marriages showed that a number of teens marry to escape an unhappy homelife or domination by their parents. Many others, uncertain about themselves and not convinced they are needed or wanted by anyone, have a compulsive need to love and to be loved. All too often this need for love is mistaken for the real thing— love for the other person.

One young man comments, "It's ludicrous how often a high schooler can fall in love forever." Maybe. But it's not funny. It's a very painful part of growing up.

And it's something else. It's a pretty compelling reason why *whatever* you do that is justified "because we're in love" ought to be thought about a little bit more!

There's love—and love

That's another loophole. It is not *affection* that makes *anything* right. When someone gives "We love each other" as explanation for *any* behavior, he's got to ask himself, "What do I mean by love?"

It's easy to mix love up with loving feelings. Our emotions, our sensations, all the feelings that flood over us and convince us we're in love are too often misread as love itself. In one sense this is love. Love certainly should involve our whole personalities since we are whole persons. It's hard to conceive of a proposal of marriage delivered in a cold, dispassionate tone, accepted after thoughtful consideration of the pros and cons, and sealed with a hand-shake! Somehow we feel "love" shouldn't be so calculating.

Love shouldn't be just calculating. But love shouldn't be just feeling either. Biblically love is portrayed as a far more complete commitment. "If you love someone, you will be loyal to him no matter what the cost," Paul writes. Such loyalty doesn't depend on feelings. It can't rest on a foundation of sensations and emotions because these change. Love that's loyal, "for better or for worse," has to flow from the total character of the lover. It has to rest on purpose and resolve that reflect a total commitment to seek only the best for the one loved.

This is the kind of love the Bible talks of when it says God loves, and gave His Son. It's this kind of love people are talking about when they say love makes something right. Not our feelings, but our intention to do what is best for the other. They say we should sacrifice ourselves, if need be, for the other person's good.

Somehow it's hard to believe that this is the love fellows and girls talk about when they use "love" to explain dating behavior. Not that they don't honestly feel affection for each other. They probably do. It's just that it's hard to believe they've thought honestly about what's *best* for each other.

Many kids see physical expression of affection (ranging from kissing and necking through petting to intercourse) as a way to show affection and to build their relationship. It doesn't always work out this way. "Instead of strengthening," says one girl, "it only weakens the relationship." For every teen who believes that intimate physical involvement does strengthen a couple's relationship, there seem to be several who disagree. Remember Gene's reaction to making out and petting with a girl he'd dated for two and a half years? "It's bothering me so much," he confessed, "that I can't even kiss her good night anymore without thinking about this type of thing. What can I do?"

Neither Gene nor his girlfriend expected this result or wanted it for the other. But it happened.

A California fellow added his story:

I knew the Lord (my girl friend did too), but Jan and I began to let the barriers down. At first it was just a lot of kissing, but then it got into french kissing and petting. It became an accustomed thing for me to expect from her. I left the Lord out of my life because of this, and this was all I lived for. God changed this: He broke it up. Today I am ashamed of the way I acted. I changed Jan's life and mine. We thought it was "different" for us because we loved each other.

My girl friend wasn't as lucky as I. After breaking up I got close to the Lord, but she met an unsaved guy and they're planning to get married. She came to me about four months after we broke up and cried her eyes out. She knows she's away from the Lord, and doesn't know how to get back. I didn't know what to say. I pray for her every day now.

It just isn't worth the grief to get too familiar before marriage.

There's love—and there's love. Maybe you don't just *think* you're different. Maybe you really do love each other. But if it's real love you won't want to get your fellow into a fix like Gene's, or your girl into a mess like Jan's.

Now, don't take this for "scare technique." It isn't. Some kids seem quite happy with deep sexual involvement. But it doesn't always work out that way. And a love that looks out for the other person doesn't take chances.

That's why I said a while ago it was hard to believe that kids who say, "But we love each other" really mean *love*. If a boy urged his girl to walk a high wire, commenting, "Aw, there's only one chance in ten you'll fall and be maimed for life," I'd start wondering if he really loved her. Personally, I find it awfully hard to believe that the "love" of a couple who take chances with each other's lives can be very deep. It may exist as affection. But is it really love?

It's different for us

There's another reason for the feeling that it's different for us than for all the Genes and Jans. Deeper even than the conviction that the love we feel is the real, the total, the commitment-level thing. The reason is that emotionally we've bought the idea that no one can say what's right or wrong for anyone else. That, in fact, a person can't even know himself until he's in the situation where the choice has to be made.

One girl quoted earlier wrote, "Maybe for other couples who are really in love premarital sex is all right. Because I don't think anyone should have anything to say except the couple themselves."

Another girl agrees: "If others feel more freely about sex it is their prerogative. For them it is right, for me it is wrong."

This is a big question. Can something be wrong for me, yet right for you?

It's obvious that the answer to this one is yes. It would be wrong for me to attempt brain surgery. It would be all right for brain surgeon. The fact that I don't know a clamp from a suture makes it pretty clear that if a surgeon and I were standing together in an operating room, *he* should take the scalpel, and I should take off. But for basic moral questions, the answer isn't so obvious.

The Bible makes some pretty definite statements about sex. "Don't get involved in sex sin" is stated about as absolutely as possible. Our task, is to discover not whether sex sin is wrong (it is), or whether love makes it right (it doesn't), but to determine just what constitutes sex sin.

And love isn't the only factor the Bible considers!

Where does love come in? First, in our motives. Just knowing what's right or what's best for ourselves and others doesn't mean we'll do it—particularly when we've got some overpowering personal motives not to! If we really love, our personal motives (whether pleasure, a need to feel loved, or whatever) will be set aside for the sake of the other. Real love motivates that kind of decision, in and out of marriage.

A second way love enters in is in God's character and will. If God *has* set standards that we're to follow, He didn't do it in order to frustrate us! His motive for giving them was love. Intelligent love. While we may not know what our actions can do to ourselves and others, He does. He knows us, and He knows the pathway that leads to real depth of relationship, and to real joy in all His gifts.

Unanswered questions

There are many questions to be answered. Where *does* physical expression of affection fit in? What's right for dating? Between steadies? For engaged couples and in marriage?

In one sense, we're no closer than before to defining how far we can go and why. We will look at these questions closely. But it has been important to take a look at the "we're in love" school of sexual freedom. Why?

Love is so important—to girls. Or, especially to girls. "Any guy knows," says an Indiana fellow, "that if he tells a girl he loves her she'll be more willing to neck. For many guys it's become a game, if not a fine art."

The need to be loved puts tremendous pressure on girls in their dating relationships. One study showed what all the girls, and most of the guys, already know. Girls' " 'wrong behavior' on a date usually occurs because of fears they will not be liked if they do not participate."²

This says a lot to both guys and girls. If she ought to be aware of his physical makeup and avoid turning her man on, he ought to be just as aware of her emotional makeup and avoid talking loosely about love. "The fact is," says an Iowa teen, "contrary to the beliefs of many 'experts,' that a boy who is out with a girl who really cares for and respects him can, over a period of time, maneuver her almost any way he desires."

Maybe a fellow isn't consciously trying to maneuver his girl when he says, "I love you." But pretty soon he catches on to the power of this little phrase and begins to throw it around loosely. It's a real temptation, that's for sure. But anyone who is concerned about his date and not himself will watch it!

"Love" doesn't always mean love. That's something everyone has to remember. Love may be just a word we use to describe those chills and quivers we get when we're with our dates. Or love may be just a word we try to use (like a key) to unlock the cupboard to goodies we want for ourselves.

This is important for girls to consider. When a boy says, "I love you" he *may* mean "I love *me* and want something from you!" This is the way a lot of boys use it.

How can you tell? Here are some simple tests of hidden motives: Did he start telling you he "loved" you on the first date? When does he say it—when you're alone in the car and he starts to reach for you? Does he tie his expressions of love to demands that you "prove" your love for him? Does he use love to excuse something you (or he) feel guilty about? A "yes" to any of these means that the chances are what he's talking about isn't *love*; at least not the caring, commitment kind of love you yearn for.

And remember this too: Guys who really respect a girl

and think highly of her don't start off their relationship with talk about love, and a demand for physical expression of affection. You wouldn't sell your body for money. So why exchange it for three little words?

Real love demands as well as frees. That's probably the biggest thing about "We love each other." The depth of love isn't measured by the freedom taken but by the responsibility exercised.

Love never is valid as an excuse for any behavior. When we talk of it that way, what we're talking about is just feelings. A love that's concerned about what's best for the other person doesn't take chances and doesn't need excuses.

Probably this is why you've read this far. You *do* care. About yourself. About your girl friend. Or your boyfriend. If you do care, don't fall into the trap of thinking that "love" makes everything different for you, that you can do what you wouldn't think right for others because you're in love.

You can never *know* until you marry whether he or she is the one. And you can't tell beforehand what effect your actions might have on the personality of your date, upon your relationship with each other or upon your fellowship with God.

Somehow we all have to look beyond love to find the right thing to do. For whatever part love plays in sanctifying sex, love can't do it alone.

Steps to take

1. Look over the quotes in this chapter, and note how the guys and girls used the word "feel." What does this say to you about the way they think of love?

2. How do you think a person can tell real love? How can a person tell if another is really in love with him? Jot down your ideas.

3. Here are some more biblical passages to compare. What do these passages say to you?
   > 1 Corinthians 10:11-13
   > 1 Corinthians 13
   > Jeremiah 7:19-20; 23-28

4. If you are dating steadily, try to honestly define the kind of "love" you have between you. Write down the evidence for your conclusion.

5

God invented sex

When asked what he thought the biblical view of sex is, one Christian teen objected, "The Bible is not a sex text." In one sense he's right. It's not a text, in the sense of a how-to manual. It's not a text in the sense of giving rules for every kind of behavior either. But underneath all the questions that tug for the attention of teens and those in their twenties, such as "What, specifically, can I do?" and "What, specifically, can't I do?" lie far more basic questions.

"I feel," writes a sophomore girl, "that most high schoolers don't really understand sex, its implications, and its role in life." That's quite clear from our first four chapters. Some saw sex as purchasing power; something with which to buy their way to acceptance. Some found the fun philosophy appealing, and couldn't get sex off the animal-pleasure level. Even those who wanted to fit sex into a love relationship didn't see the whole picture.

Sex is puzzling even when you understand God's purpose in creating it. It's positively painful when you build your life on a distorted view. "I used to think it was sinful, even in marriage," one girl reported. That attitude doesn't square with the biblical picture—and it surely would make marriage difficult for her and her future husband! But the seventeen-year-old who wrote about going all the way and said, "I think that making love is good and that if people love each other it is OK because it is human nature and God wanted it" is just as far off.

How do such misunderstandings arise, and why does it seem so difficult to develop clear-cut standards, supported by solid biblical reasons? Many of the questions kids ask aren't answered directly in the Bible. For example, look at some of the toughies high school and college kids threw out when they contributed their ideas for this book.

Why did God create sex? Are the rules for sexual behavior cut and dried? What constitutes marriage—sexual intercourse itself, the ceremony, or what? What is the purpose and meaning of marriage? Why do some people say petting outside of marriage is "selfish," but that in marriage the same thing is loving? What's the difference between love and lust? What makes sexual desire "love" in marriage and "lust" outside of it? How do you reconcile Bible history with church teaching on marriage? Are our desires sinful in themselves?

Did somebody goof?

This is perhaps the first thing to get straight. God didn't goof when He invented sex.

Those feelings that well up in guys and gals as they mature sexually, those pleasant sensations associated with the sexually sensitive areas of our bodies—all were built in by God on purpose. He planted the nerve endings in men and women. He arranged for kissing, for touch-

ing, for petting and for intercourse to be exciting and pleasurable.

"God created man in his own image," Genesis 1:27 (RSV) reports, "male and female he created them." And thus the Bible speaks of sex without embarrassment: "The man and his wife were both naked, and were not ashamed" (Gen. 2:25 RSV). While it may be, and is, a shame to speak of sex as so many do today, sex isn't shameful or secular; it's sacred. And the Bible is open about it, honestly portraying both its joyous experience and its misuse.

It's hard for us to think of sex as "sacred," as something we can talk about openly before God. As something husbands and wives can experience naturally and without guilt. Certainly sex is private. It's between two people.

Two people and God. But within that context every sensation, every pleasure, every experience is pleasing to us
and to Him. What was God's evaluation after creating
man? Was it the same as His reaction to creating the world
or the animal kingdom: "And . . . it was good"? No,
when God created man, male and female, He looked at
them in their total being and in their essential sexuality:
"And . . . it was *very* good" (Gen. 1:31 RSV).

How do we get the idea then that sex is something to be
swept under the rug? Sort of a dirty necessity, an animal
function that's built in because to reproduce we just have
to go through with it?

The source is the peculiar idea that we and our bodies
are separate. That an immaterial "real us" is just temporarily stuck with an animated hunk of clay.

This really isn't the biblical picture of man. We're *not*
composed of isolated and incompatible functions (like
body and soul) welded together by some magic only God
could perform. Sure, the Bible does speak of our body,
soul and spirit. But we've mixed up the way the Bible uses
these terms with the way Western philosophers have used
them.

For instance, what impression do you get when you
read the phrase "sins of the flesh"? Drunkenness? Sex
sin? Maybe gluttony or drugs? Things that have their root
in the physical characteristics and appetites of a person?
Well, if that's what flesh means, how does Paul get such
*non*physical things as strife, jealousy, anger, selfishness
and envy into his lists of "sins of the flesh" in Galatians 5?
These just don't fit our sterotype of "flesh" at all.

Actually, we tend to think of ourselves much like the
blind men who tried to describe an elephant. Remember?
One felt the tail and said the elephant was like a snake.
Another felt the leg and concluded it was like a tree trunk.

Others felt the flat ear, the flexible trunk, the tusks, etc. Each gave his description, but the picture was wrong because it was based on only one aspect of the elephant *out of relationship to the whole*. You must see the whole.

It's the same with us. We can't think of our "sex life" as something apart from our total life. Or of what we do with our bodies as something apart from *us*: what we are and what we will become. The Bible doesn't slice man up this way. The Bible uses words like "flesh" and "spirit" to show us ourselves as wholes—but from different angles.

What's the angle when we look at ourselves as "flesh"? In the Old Testament the angle is man as a person living in the real world. In the New Testament an ethical dimension is emphasized. Man is living in the world, but estranged from God, caught in a web of sin within and without. That's why a "sin of the flesh" can be envy as well as adultery. "Flesh" reminds us that, apart from God, we're lost. It says, "Here's how men act in this world, separated from God."

All such terms—body, soul, spirit, heart, mind—have their own emphases, their own angles. But none slices up human personality. None looks at the physical (or the "spiritual") apart from the whole person, the whole life.

This is extremely important. It's basic. Why? Because our *wholeness* doesn't permit us to pass off sex as something "just physical." It's not our bodies that lust; it's us. It's not our bodies that blend in marital embrace; it's us. Any sexual act brings our total personality into play. So sex can't be just something to *use*—like sports cars and TV and bank accounts. To understand sex, we have to see it in the context of our total selves—and in the context of sex's necessary impact on the total personality of the other person involved.

Role of relationships

When Adam was first created the Bible portrays him as
alone—and uneasy. He named the cattle, Genesis 2:20
(rsv) tells us. "But for the man there was not found a
helper fit for [suited to] him." It was then that the Lord
caused Adam to sleep, and fashioned Eve from his rib.
When God brought her to him, the man recognized her as
essential to himself; "This . . . is bone of my bones and
flesh of my flesh." And God added this commentary:
"Therefore a man leaves his father and his mother and
cleaves to his wife, and they become one flesh" (Gen.
2:23-24 rsv). Why the "therefore"? Because we need in
our deepest selves a personal closeness which family can
satisfy in a child, *but which only a "oneness" relationship
between the sexes can satisfy in the adult.*

It's helpful to remember here that "one flesh" is not
merely the physical aspect of marriage. "Flesh" in the Old
Testament draws our attention to the whole man in his
life on earth. In marriage a man and a woman commit
themselves to each other on every level of personality,
including (but *not only*) the physical. In Christ's words,
they are "no longer two, but one!" And, He added, "God
has joined [them] together" (Matt. 19:6).

Biblically speaking, sex fits *only* in the context of this
oneness relationship. God so blended our bodies with our
total selves that physical self-giving is sensed as the seal
of total commitment. It's a very real and unmistakable
way of saying, "I am *totally* yours."

Within the framework of such a relationship intercourse is wholly good, and the physical pleasures a man
and woman find in each other amplify and confirm their
sense of commitment and joy in each other. Outside of
this relationship, sex is a distortion of the divine plan. It's

a use of the body and a use of sex as an _end_ to gain personal pleasure. But sex was designed as a _means_ of assisting in the development of that most intimate of all human relationships between husband and wife.

So God invented sex, and He didn't goof. He built in all those exciting and pleasant sensations—and He wants you to enjoy them. But sex isn't an end, it's a means. You are a whole person, not an entity with a body to use, as you'd use a TV, for entertainment. Your body is you. (So much so that God plans a resurrection. We couldn't be ourselves in eternity, 1 Cor. 15 suggests, if God weren't planning to reshape our present bodies into resurrection bodies.)

This identity of you with your body means that the physical you is so intimately interwoven with the emotional and psychological and spiritual you that it's impossible to separate them. Each affects the other, and each is affected by the other. This interrelatedness is, in a way, the patent protection God built into His invention of sex. It makes sure that we can't use sex to take rather than to give. It makes sure that no one can use sex outside of the marriage "oneness" relationship and find meaning and fulfillment.

What happens when we use sex to _take_? The cries for help of some of the teens and those in their twenties quoted earlier point to one of God's built-in patent protections. These kids didn't know what was right or wrong about what they did, but they didn't _feel_ right about it. They felt guilty. Call it what you want: "icky," one girl called it. It still boils down to guilt.

Today lots of college and high school students feel they're freed from all the hang-ups of the older generation. They believe that the morals, rules and standards of mom and dad brought only frustration, and that they themselves should now live freed of such repressions, joyous and guiltless. But Dr. S. L. Halleck, professor of psychiatry at Wisconsin University, who has worked intensively with students, says that such a person "in his belief that life and especially the sexual aspects of life can be enjoyed without guilt becomes highly disturbed when he discovers that . . . a certain amount of guilt is inevitable."[1] That's just it. A certain amount of guilt, a nagging sense of alienation, *is* inevitable.

What about the idea that the sexually promiscuous person is "liberated" and free to get to know several persons well, not just restricted to a depth relationship with one?

Recently Dr. Theodore Isaac Rubin, another well-known psychiatrist, answered a person who asked if the somewhat sexually promiscuous woman is more sophisticated and liberated than the woman who is not. His answer:

> Psychiatrically speaking, if they were sexually liberated, they would not be promiscuous—somewhat or otherwise. Promiscuity is a function of anxiety. It is a symptom. The sexually promiscuous person is choicelessly driven from one partner to another, in an effort to feel less anxious. Sex for her has little to do with relatedness and invariably proves to be disappointing. The promiscuous people I have seen in treatment were usually anything but sophisticated or liberated. These terms are hardly suitable to describe what is really an effort to rationalize unresolved infantile yearnings; a strong need to rebel against authority, and an overpowering and very conventional conscience; an extremely immature sexual outlook; and a marked inability to sustain a mature relationship on any level—especially the sexual level.

> In my opinion, a woman must be capable of an exclusive, sustained, involved (investing emotions and caring about) heterosexual relationship, to be liberated and sophisticated sexually.[2]

What the doctor is saying, and what psychiatry is making more and more plain, is that the Bible has been right all along.

God invented sex for marriage, for a total, sustained and exclusive man-woman relationship. In this kind of relationship we can mature as individuals, and two people can grow together as the "one" the Bible says they are.

Outside of this relationship sex simply won't work.

Oh, you can get the surface thrills, the physical excitement—for a time. But since you are more than your body, the depths can never be yours. And the day will come when you'll fit into Dr. Rubin's description of the sexually "liberated" person of today—anxious, full of unresolved infantile yearnings, unable to sustain a mature relationship—and to top it off you'll find that this kind of sex life is "invariably disappointing."

No, the Bible isn't a sex text. But it does give us the straight scoop. It gives us the inside information on who we are, what sexuality is, and why God made us male and female.

Even men who try to live like goats discover that the God they deny built sex into their personalities for a purpose, and simply won't let that purpose be perverted without full payment. God's patent protection works.

Steps to take

1. In this chapter we've looked at the broad outlines of the biblical view of sex. Before we get into details, check over the questions which you wrote down after reading chapter 1. Do you see answers to any of them suggested in this chapter?

2. Two Bible passages sharply portray sex within and outside of God's intended purpose. If you'd care to read them, they're the Song of Solomon and Romans 1:18-32.

6

Freedom now!

The word "law" is a funny one. It's got overtones that we don't often spell out, but that no one really misses. These can color our view of the Bible and may discolor our view of the rights and wrongs God spells out for us.

For instance, one overtone of law is "restriction." We almost all automatically relate law to "can't," not to "can." We think of all the things law keeps us from doing, things that often seem quite appealing. Who hasn't driven up to a red light late at night, seen no one for miles, and wondered, "Why not?" We know it would be safe, but somehow the law bothers us, and we feel we ought to obey it anyway.

Almost all rules work like this at times. They stand as a barrier between us and something we want to do. And we're so bugged by rules then. Sometimes we keep them, even though we can't really see why we should except that we feel we ought to. Sometimes we break them, and there's a little nagging sense of doing something wrong.

No, rules aren't pleasant. They
often frustrate us or make us feel
guilty. And neither of these feelings is
pleasant.

It's easy to transfer this feeling of an-
noyance to the people who make the
laws and rules. Parents, campus author-
ity, our town or city, the country—even
God—have come in for their share of criticism. The thing
that hurts most is the feeling that often we're in a better
position than the law-makers to know what would work
out. For instance, at the traffic light. We know it's there to
regulate traffic, but right now there *isn't* any traffic.
Really, what's the sense of just waiting for it to turn?

And so pretty soon the whole area of laws and restrictions gets mixed up with this sense of unreasonableness—this idea that the lawmakers don't really know the situation like you do and, really, ought to butt out!

It's tough when these attitudes carry over into our relationship with God and the Bible. Because here, at least, feelings of resentment just don't square with the facts. When God says He wants us to do something or not to do something His purpose isn't to frustrate us. It's to free us. And He does know what's going on—even in this modern world.

Some of the teens quoted earlier were looking for freedom. "Frankly speaking, I found it most difficult to distinguish what was right from what was wrong and why." "High schoolers wonder what is right and what is wrong because they see *so many* doing what they are told is wrong. Many Christian teenagers want *reasons* for not going out and doing what the other couples do." The kids don't want to do anything that will be harmful to them emotionally, physically, spiritually—but most of the time the only way they can find out what is harmful is the hard way. I don't mean a girl gets pregnant necessarily. I just mean they do something—anything—that seems to them a little off-color afterward, and thus makes them feel uncomfortable with themselves and each other."

See the freedom they want? Not freedom to go ahead until you find out the hard way, but freedom to *know* beforehand what helps and what is going to harm. It's no fun to stand there uncertain, wondering what to do.

All the law is, to some extent, freeing. But God's laws are totally freeing. That is, their deepest purpose is not to restrict but to guide into the kind of life that will bring us the greatest joy, meaning and fulfillment. Anyone who has "thought it was different for us" or who has "thought

it was out of love" and discovered he was wrong knows
we need guidance. We need the kind of guidelines that
will tell us ahead of time what will harm us and what will
help.

So let's look at some of the rules that go along with the
Bible's presentation of the purpose of sex. And let's see if
the pathway to freedom will begin to open up for us.

Legalized sex?

"I think," says a young college girl, "that marriage
ought to be defined. Why wait if the wedding ceremony is
just the OK signal from society to have sexual intercourse?"

It's a pretty good question. Especially since so many of
God's restrictions on sex are related to marriage. Is marriage really just society's way of legalizing sex? If so, a
ceremony certainly doesn't make two people one. For instance, take a look at the Hollywood personalities who
have worked their way through a whole series of husbands or wives. Did the fact that they had a paper saying
they'd gone through a ceremony with each of them in turn
make them married? Hardly!

Remember the Genesis passage we looked at in the last
chapter? "Therefore," it says, "a man leaves his father and
his mother and cleaves to his wife, and they become one
flesh." Here we have the hallmarks of marriage; and there
is more than intercourse involved.

You have grown and matured in your home—to a
point. But a time is coming when your relationship with
your parents can no longer meet your needs. You'll need
an even more intimate relationship with someone else.
This is the underlying reason for God's invention of sexuality, that in the oneness experienced by a man and
woman the deepest needs of each could be met.

What, then, is it that binds two people in this relationship? Three conditions:

1. You "leave" father and mother. Your dependence on your parents is gradually lessened, until emotionally, financially, etc., you are no longer a child. You step out on your own.

2. You "cleave" to your wife (or husband). None of us is truly independent. None of us lives healthily apart from relationship with other human beings. Sometimes, its' true, a man or a woman remains unmarried. But still such a person needs friends, companions, others with whom to talk and share and about whom to be concerned. Probably you will find a person with whom you want to establish the closest relationship possible. And with the intention of establishing a permanent home (for this is the implication of "cleave"), you will join your life to him or her.

3. Your intention is sealed by the total giving of yourself to each other in sexual intercourse. You two will become "one flesh."

And *then* you'll be married.

It's important to keep all three of these in mind: leaving home, intention to establish a new home, sexual intercourse. When the Bible warns us to "marry in holiness and honor—not in lustful passion as the heathen do," it's making it very clear that marriage isn't to be just a license for sex. While sexual desire for the one you love isn't wrong (far from it!), the underlying motive must not be a self-indulgent desire to *use* another person, but a desire to establish and to build a oneness relationship with him.

Where does the ceremony fit in? That's not too clear yet. But certainly it ought to be clear that every society has some way of marking publicly the intention of two people to establish a home. Maybe it's just drinking tea from the

same cup before witnesses; perhaps as in Bible days it's
exchanging vows (cf. Heb. 13:4). Or as in our day, standing before a minister and promising to love, honor and
cherish each other. Each of these is a public expression of
intention to establish a home. And as such it's important.

Why important? For one thing, the Bible says, "Be de-
cent and true in everything you do so that all can approve
your behavior" (Rom. 13:13). What other people see and
think is important. But a public ceremony also focuses for
us the kind of commitment marriage demands. When we
say, "I want to marry you" we ought to be saying far more
than "I have a certain affection for you and would like to
express it sexually." We ought to be saying, "I'm ready to
commit my total self to you for my whole life." That's
saying a lot more than "I love you."

And saying it publicly means more than saying it pri-
vately, at night, parked in some dark car. In the dark alone
even "Will you marry me?" may mean "Will you let me
enjoy your body now?" But standing right up there before
witnesses, signing legal documents and publicly exchanging vows says, "I intend, God helping me, to commit myself to you and live my whole life with you."

And so the public ceremony becomes in a sense the
only real proof we can offer another person of the sincerity
of our intention to be really married—not just our intention to enjoy sex.

"You were united to your wife by the Lord," Malachi
says. "When you married, the two of you became one
person in His sight" (2:15). And you will become one
person only when sexual intercourse is the private con-
summation of a publicly stated intention to establish a
new home.

What about—premarital intercourse? What about divorce? What about adultery?

The biblical position on each is simple. All are prohibited. But not to restrict us, or keep us from something good and enjoyable. They're restricted so that we might be free to enjoy the full meaning of sex within marriage.

"Rejoice," the Bible encourages us, "in the wife of your youth, a lovely hind, a graceful doe. Let her affection fill you at all times with delight, be infatuated always with her love" (Prov. 5:18-19 RSV).

Sadly, God's restrictive laws didn't always lead His people into the relationship He had planned for them. The Bible records cases in which even saints stepped out of line. Some had multiple wives. (If you've ever thought of that as an ideal state, you might read Genesis 25–35. The friction and jealousy these chapters record, and the favoritism Jacob displayed, might help change your impression!)

But for all the variations in *practice*, God's intentions for marriage remained consistently the same. The Pharisees once objected to Christ's condemnation of divorce and asked, "Why then did Moses command one to give a certificate of divorce, and to put her away?" Christ answered, "For your hardness of heart Moses allowed you to divorce your wives, but from the beginning it was not so. And I say to you: whoever divorces his wife, except for unchastity, and marries another, commits adultery" (Matt. 19:7-9 RSV).

Whatever the Bible records about historic practices, it's not there as a model or as justification for our behavior, but because the Bible accurately reports what happened. What is God's intention for us is clear—clearly stated in the Old Testament, and clearly restated by Christ Himself in the New.

The Bible does state a number of freeing rules concerning sex. All point us toward the real meaning of sex and the full enjoyment of it found in marriage. But the Bible leaves a lot unsaid that some of us would like spelled out. More than one correspondent asked "Please spell out *exactly* what we can do, and what we can't do."

It is clear from Scripture that we can't "go all the way." Premarital (and that does mean before *marriage*) intercourse is wrong. Adultery is wrong. But the Bible doesn't say anything about such practices as necking. Or petting—light or heavy. Because Scripture doesn't say we *can't*, dare we infer that we *can*? That anything and everything except intercourse is all right outside of marriage? Or that it's all right "if we love each other"?

These are questions that are going to take the rest of the book to answer. But there are some basic concepts that will help us find answers.

Commitment, not "love," is at issue. Sex was created by God to express the totality of our commitment to one person. Certainly we're to "love" that person. The Bible says, "Husbands, love your wives" (Eph. 5:25 RSV).

But then we're to *love* everyone! "Let love guide your life," says Colossians 3:14. "Love your neighbor as [much as you love] yourself" (Lev. 19:18) is a well-known and much quoted command. Christ made it even tougher with this teaching: "You have heard that it was said, 'You shall love your neighbor and hate your enemy.' But I say to you, Love your enemies and pray for those who persecute you" (Matt. 5:43-44 RSV).

How are we supposed to love our neighbor and our enemies? Sexually? Of course not. There are many ways to show love for others. We're to care about their welfare. We're to help them in their needs. If a fellow or girl is cut out of your group, you can become a friend and help them in. This is "love"—this looking out for the other person because you're concerned about him. And it's clear that this kind of love isn't necessarily associated with sex.

But, you may be thinking, that's not the kind of "love" we mean when we talk about a man and woman. What we're talking about is affection—love feelings.

But that's just it! As we saw in chapter 4, *affection* doesn't make *anything* right. God didn't create sex so that we could show affection.

Now, there's nothing wrong with showing affection. It's just that it's not necessary (or called for) to always show affection with sex.

Look at it this way. Most of us "fall in love" with several boys or girls before we settle down to marriage. We feel a real—a special—affection for each of them—for a while. But we also fall out of love with most of them. We may still love them in the sense of feeling concern. We're supposed to. But that special affection dies or changes. Someday, though, we meet one person with whom we decide to join lives. We burn all the bridges and stand up before witnesses and promise to love him "till death do us part." And then, with *this* person, sex seems necessary, appropriate and right.

God didn't create sex to show affection. He invented it to seal commitment. And outside of this context of total commitment, sex just doesn't fit.

Motives are important. Sex, as we've seen earlier, is tied in with self-giving. It's not an end in itself, but a means.

Whenever we ask, What is right? or What is wrong? we can never answer with a simple list of dos and don'ts. Sometimes even *looking* at a girl is wrong! You can read it in Matthew 5:28: "Every one who looks at a woman lustfully has already committed adultery with her in his heart." (RSV).

Notice the key word here: "lustfully." It's not wrong to appreciate beauty, but it is wrong to think of a girl as a thing to use. Even to see another person as something to *get* is sin.

Sometimes we ask, "What is definitely wrong?" and really mean, "How far can I go in using another person to gratify my own desires and passions?" The answer in this case is clear. You can never use another person *at all* and be right. It's always wrong, whatever it is.

The Bible says a definite "Stop!" to premarital intercourse and to adultery partly because it's inconceivable that we could ever enter into this kind of relationship with wholly pure motives. Sex is inherently a sign of total commitment. When we use it outside that framework we're using it for self-gratification.

Don't misunderstand my use of "self-gratification" here. Don't think it's just related to raw physical sensation. Self-gratification is also behind such hidden motives as giving yourself because you're afraid that you won't be accepted otherwise, or taking because "everybody's doing it."

In all such cases, sex is being used to get. The motive is wrong. And whatever is done from a wrong motive *is* wrong.

God does care

In this chapter we've looked at some of God's rules and restrictions concerning sex, and have suggested that they are designed to free, not to frustrate. When we do what God wants, we find that His will leads us out of doubt, fear and guilt into a confident enjoyment of life.

This is a healthy and distinctively Christian way to look at all the Bible's moral teachings. The Scripture has a gospel of abundant life as well as a gospel of eternal life. Both news of Christ's death for us sinners and news of His will for our daily lives are gospel: good news.

Sometimes we lost sight of this. Then we're frustrated by the nagging feeling that we *ought* to do something we really don't want to do. It's true that we often want to do things we shoudn't. That's part of what it means to be a sinner. The good news of God's will for us is that by looking to Him and obeying Him, even when we're inclined toward a different course of action, we can be sure the peace and joy the Bible speaks of will be ours. Sure, a decision to restrict ourselves might hurt now. But the same decision will help us avoid far greater hurt, pain and guilt later on.

Whatever God says we *ought* to do is for our good, not because He's capriciously enforcing His own unreasonable ideas on "poor little us."

There is another side to God's will too. Stepping out of it isn't just unwise. It's sin. God's Old Testament people wearied Him, the Bible says, by saying that "evil is good, that it pleases the Lord! or by saying that God won't punish us—He doesn't care" (Mal. 2:17).

God does care. He cares about you and me too much to let us knowingly step out of His will and go undisciplined. As far as our sex life is concerned, the Bible is quite blunt: "Sexual sin is never right: our bodies were not made for that, but for the Lord, and the Lord wants to fill our bodies with Himself (1 Cor. 6:13). "That is why," the passage goes on, "I say run from sex sin. No other sin affects the body as this one does. When you sin this sin it is against your own body. Haven't you yet learned that your body is the home of the Holy Spirit God gave you, and that He lives within you? Your own body does not belong to you, for God has bought you with a great price. So use every part of your body to give glory back to God, because He owns it" (1 Cor. 6:18-20).

In these next chapters we're going to look at the in-between things—at dating, petting, steadies and engagement—and give you a chance in each of these areas to discover and develop whatever restrictions will lead you to assurance of freedom.

Funny, isn't it, how odd these two—freedom and restrictions—look together. But if what you want is freedom to know what will help and what will hurt, freedom from the danger of going too far (whatever "too far" may be), freedom to find and enjoy God's very best, then you have to set, and keep, limits.

Only within these limits can you be free.

Steps to take

1. In what way are "love" and "commitment" related in marriage?

2. A passage related to the freeing nature of obedience is Romans 6:11-23. What does this passage say to you?

3. Look back over your own dating experience. What restrictions, if followed, might have freed you from something you now see as harmful or guilt-producing? Jot them down, then relate them to the ideas summarized in the "said—and unsaid" section of this chapter.

7

Getting to know you

It's funny how dating starts. All the uncertain, exciting feelings a person may have on that all-important "first." Somehow dating isn't all tied up with sex, then.

Here's how one of my students at Wheaton College described very graphically a girl's first excursion into the realm of dating:

Great Scott, is this hair or a wire mop? Where's the hair spray? It's got to be here somewhere. I know it does. Oh. Here it is.

There. Now to see how the back looks. Oh no, I've sprayed it and there's a strand out of place. Let's see. That's better. Now for the lipstick. What a ghastly color! Better use my sister's. She won't mind. Hope he doesn't notice that my eye liner is thinner in some places than others. If I'd only been more careful in using that eyelash curler. I wouldn't be minus half of one eyelash. It makes the other eyelid feel heavier.

Now, let's see. What about the whole effect? This sweater looks a bit—

The doorbell! Oh no. I'm sick. I can't go.

Well, now that I'm in the car, how close to him should I
sit? What will he think if I squeeze over a few more in-
ches? Make it casual. Act like you know what you're
doing.

Sniff, sniff. What kind of shaving lotion does he have
on? Wonder if he really does need to shave. Can't tell in
this light. He has nice eyelashes. Hope he likes my per—
Perfume! I forgot to put on my perfume! Oh, no. Disaster.

Guess I'd better start praying that my deodorant holds.

For Pete's sake! I've run out of topics. He's going to
think I'm an awful bore. Quick! Think of something,
anything.

Great Scott! Now I sound like a babbling fool. Shut up,
you idiot.

Good. Food at last? It looks like a nice place. Well, out
we go. Oops. I think I should have let him open that door.
Why can't I remember what I'm supposed to do? What
must he think of me? Oh, no. I ran my nylon getting out of
that confounded car. I can feel it creeping up the back of
my leg. Nothing like a chic appearance! Smile. Smile.
Smile!

Help, What do I order? I've no idea what to spend.
These prices are ridiculous. I know. Order what he does.
That's the girl. You're catching on. Remember, this is fun.
Fun.

What did he just say? I think it was funny. Laugh.
Laugh! Oh, no. Stop laughing. You're choking on your
food. What if I cough it all over the table? A glass of water.
Quick! Where's the water?

I'm afraid I don't look very ladylike.

Don't eat too much—he'll think you're some kind of
pig.

I can tell he's not having a good time. Actually, he's a
very nice boy. I guess. I wish I knew him.

Well, time to leave. Ahhhhh— Ha-ha! Thought you
were going to fall over that chair, didn't you? Your grace
and poise are amazing.

Oh no, it's raining. My hair and—my coat! This material *stinks* when it gets wet! I think I'm going to die. Nothing like going out with a garbage can.

Oh, why did I come? Why? At least we're on the way home now. Guess I've done all the damage I can. I'll be so glad to say good night. Say good night? Oh no. What is he—

But he wouldn't. Would he? Why didn't I think of this before? You goose, what did you think you'd do, shake hands? But I couldn't—I just couldn't! I wouldn't know how! Somebody help me. Here we are!

Slam. What a relief! It's over. Hallelujah! I hope it was all right to just thank him for the evening and then come in. Hope I didn't look like I was in a hurry. What if he thought I was afraid of him? He'll think it was the first time I was out—that I'm inexperienced or something. No! He couldn't.

He was nice though. Had strong hands and arms. And he did say that he'd see me again.

Maybe next time. . . .

An important step

Read any psychology text on young people, and you'll find the author talks a lot about the developmental tasks of adolescence—the adjustments each of us has to make as we mature. Among them you'll always find this: a need to learn to socialize, with an emphasis on building heterosexual friendships. As if we didn't already know!

It is important to learn to live in a world of two sexes. That's the way life is, and always will be. Dating isn't only a method of mate selection in our culture, it's a way of learning how to get along in a two-sexed world. It's a big step in finding ourselves and understanding ourselves in our roles as men and women.

The idea that dating is more than mate selection, that it's an important process through which we learn to relate comfortably to others in our male/female world, is a helpful one. It gives us a new slant for looking at some of the dating questions that always pop up. Take for instance the question of going steady. Let's disregard for now the argument that a "steady" relationship may lead to too much sexual intimacy (though it's been established by many studies that this is true). Let's just look at going steady from the social development angle.

A young man from Iowa who steadied all through high school and became engaged to his hometown girl, says:

> When I came to college I very suddenly realized what a lack of social education I had suffered by not dating around. This also helped me realize for the first time how insufficient intimate love is for a happy, well-rounded life. I broke our engagement, though I still love her very much.

For at present anyway neither one of us is sufficiently developed to make married life all that it can be.

This is only one side of the question, of course. There are lots of ideas as to why or why not to take a "steady" approach to dating. Put them together, and it sounds pretty confusing.

"We're in a bind. Our whole society places emphasis on going steady and only this. It's the guy who dates around that is the misfit, not vice versa. Girls are considered flirts if they skirt around and don't have a steady. Or society says, 'What's wrong with him? Isn't he stable enough to be with one person?"

"Should a guy play the field," asks an Indiana eighteen-year-old, "or go steady? Many kids want security because they lack confidence in dating. This is my problem. I keep thinking, 'The Lord will provide a date,' but I think I take dating too seriously. I'm scared to be tagged with certain girls (Christians) who boys don't think look very nice. Should one date a person if he isn't sure that person is a Christian?

"It's so hard for me to take the initiative in finding dates."

So lots of kids do go steady—to be in style, to fit in, or because they're unsure of themselves. If it's just for reasons like these that you go steady, says a sophomore girl, "it's dumb."

But what about the group that says going steady "is great! It lets two people really get to know each other." It's true. If you're really ready to concentrate on one.

When are you ready? There aren't any pat answers, but again it is a helpful idea that there's more to dating than finding your one and only. If you've dated around, and know quite a few other fellows or girls, then probably you're in a good position to recognize that "just right" one. If you've just grabbed the first warm body that toddled by, the chances are you're far more interested in your own sense of security than in him or her. Another thing to think about is this: Have you dated around enough to feel comfortable with members of the opposite sex? If not, chances are you're really going steady for that comfortable feeling that comes from being with a person who accepts and likes you.

Whatever anyone says for or against going steady, if it's a crutch, it's harmful. Dating around is the big way we learn to live in our male/female world. And who wants to be socially retarded?

Even so, I would have liked to quote more on the pro side of the issue. The only reason I haven't included more arguments in favor of going steady is this: The kids I talked with and who wrote me just didn't advance any! What nearly all seemed to feel is summed up by one older fellow: "Going steady? It's like an empty threat. If you're in love you don't need it; if you're not, it's not for you. The little security it gives is annulled by the anxiety it causes worrying about unfaithfulness and the pain when you break up."

A test case

Our brief excursion into steady dating has been just that. A test case. An example of how looking at dating as personal development rather than just mate-finding can give us a different perspective on the old familiar problems.

In dating you're really doing several things. You're learning about your own feelings and emotions as you get to know members of the opposite sex. You're learning how to relate to them as persons. You're gaining self-confidence as you develop social skills and settle down in your role as a fellow or girl. And you're sorting through a whole host of candidates for a life partner (not grabbing desperately at each one who comes along). All these things demand growth, personal devopment.

This viewpoint also helps us put sex in perspective. Dating isn't primarily getting to know others on a physical level. Our total relationship with those we date has to grow, and be kept in balance. Sure, our bodies want to get in on the act. Liking a person of the opposite sex is just naturally expressed by touch. The big question is *How much touch* makes for balanced development of the total relationship?

Growth always involves progression. Growing in relationship to a person involves progression too—on many levels. There is, for example, what we might call the *personal level.*

You meet a person who looks nice, or seems nice. You see him with the gang and note his sense of humor, the way he gets along with others, that he's fun to be with. You date, and discover that you have similar interests, similar likes and dislikes. As you get to know each other better you feel free to talk about your real feelings or your problems. You don't have to hide behind a mask with this person. You can be real. And your friendship doesn't stop here. You discover you can talk about and share spiritual experiences, get right down to the bedrock of life. And, when you're down there, you discover that you fit, that you have similar attitudes on what's important in life.

Getting to know a guy or girl on this personal level is a big thing, and complicated. It takes seeing him or her under all kinds of conditions. With the gang, working on a project, just fooling around. Sitting talking with a few other kids. Doing fun things together on dates. Talking with him or her alone; sharing the things that are interesting and important as well as those that are current and fun. Getting to know a person is far more than sitting in a car and grabbing, or being grabbed. And it's a lot more than spending all your time together, alone.

There's an *affection level* too, that keeps pace as you get to know some guys and gals.

At first it's just fun; you enjoy being together. With some people it never goes beyond this—and that's OK. You can still have fun with them. But a few you'll like better than most. If you've dated around enough to know quite a few kids casually, you'll find one or two you like better than the others. Here you're focusing in on romance, and will probably start experiencing love feelings. (It's important to remember here, though, to apply the time test. Lots of loves will probably enter your life—and exit—before you finally settle down.) In special cases the love feelings will match up with liking. You'll appreciate and respect him or her as a person, as well as feel strongly attracted. Until finally it all develops into the real thing, and you publicly commit yourself to *this* person for life.

With all this there's also the *physical level*. As I said (and as you already know!), in a developing relationship between a guy and a girl the body often wants to get in on the action. You want to touch each other; and often you want more.

There's a progression with physical contact, just as there's progression on the other levels. It often starts with holding hands. The next step is kissing, or maybe an arm around a receptive shoulder or waist. A little cuddling and necking come next. If we push the physical further, say the kids who know from experience, we move into light petting. Some go on to heavy petting. Then all that's left is intercourse.

A tightrope

It's not easy to keep life balanced, especially dating life. Our emotions are always trying to run ahead of us and convince us we're in love with a person we hardly know. And our bodies are likely to dash off too, urging us to enjoy progressively more alluring sensations with this person we "love."

The pull is natural. But that doesn't necessarily make it right or helpful. It's not even necessary to get physically involved to get to know a person well on the personal level.

An eighteen-year-old guy says:

> I feel that the most important gain from going with a girl is what can be gained from communication. That is, talking to the other person. She may be someone you can share your ambitions, fears, inhibitions, etc., with. Especially among Christian kids, you can share concepts of Christ and His love for us.

A nineteen-year-old girl from a West Coast Christian College says:

> You do not *have* to even hold hands or kiss, to prove you are in love. Dates aren't just a time to be together so you can cuddle afterwards. They're a time to get to know each other—whether having fun, doing a project, or even learning something new. It doesn't seem to depend on the physical to feel deeply for each other.

This may be hard to take. It doesn't fit the ideas of our society or our movies or magazines. But it is true. Feeling deeply for each other doesn't *depend* on the physical.

Christie, an eighteen-year-old midwesterner, writes:

> I have been going with a guy for two years, and only in the last month has the problem of sex finally been solved in a way satisfactory to me. It was always a question of

"how far can we go?" As one who has almost gone too far (by the grace of God, we didn't!) I will give my answer—which I probably wouldn't have accepted two years ago. Kissing, I now feel, is the farthest and I do not mean a passionate embrace. I don't even mean an embrace. I mean kissing, with little, if any, other bodily contact. It's just too easy to arouse a guy sexually and I think a girl should realize what she's doing to him, and for his sake not get too passionate. The thing is to never *start* going beyond what you know is right.

I would also say this. Never worry about your relationship developing too slowly. I don't really think it's possible for a relationship that may last a lifetime to develop too slowly. Take your time getting to know each other. DON'T see each other every day. Be with each other in GROUPS, not by yourselves. Don't spend all your week-end time with each other—be with other girls or guys. Get to know each other like this before there is any thought of being romantic.

And realize that guys are not the most important things in the world—there is somebody called God who is satisfying in Himself.

You may disagree with Christie. But she's been there. And back.

What does it boil down to? Thee main things.

Get the broad perspective. Dating isn't just finding a person to tag as "mine." It's a growing time for everyone. For growth to take place, for us to be comfortable with the opposite sex as well as to discover the qualities we'll want in a husband or wife, we need to know many guys or girls. Not just one or two.

And in getting to know them we should concentrate on the personal level that we mentioned earlier. Getting to know others as persons, as individuals.

This helps answer a lot of questions like "What can we do on dates?" Christie's answer was "Do lots of things—with the gang." There are other answers too.

Have fun. Good clean fun. And do things that will let you explore each other's interests and activities, your feelings and what's important to you. "I'd say," states a nineteen-year-old girl, "just enjoy yourself, and please don't try to bring sex in too early. It destroys the 'friendly' relationship one could have."

Keep the commitment context. You may not agree with Christie's reaction to too much sex in her dating life. Maybe you think more physical involvement than she advises is suitable. And you may be right.

At the same time, it's clear from Scripture that sex isn't just another way to express friendship. Or just another appetite to be satisfied. Sex was created to express commitment. Whenever sexual activity is brought into a relationship, we're saying *something* about the level of our commitment to the other person, whether we realize it or not.

Then how do you show affection? What, as one of the guys quoted in the first chapter asked, do girls expect? A junior from Illinois says, "TREAT A GIRL LIKE A GIRL! I don't know how many guys will read a book like this," she goes on, "but for those who do: please treat a girl like a *girl*. It means an awful lot to me to have any guy at any time think enough of me to treat me as a girl—for instance, open a door." Simple, sure. But when you really like a person, there are lots of ways to make it known besides sex.

Make your basic decisions now. Everyone has to make them. Why am I dating? For security? Because I'm curious and want to experiment with sex? Because I'm scared that if I don't hook my mate by seventeen I'll never make it to the altar? Or is it because I want to grow as a person, to get to know those of the opposite sex as persons, and someday to zero in on God's choice for my life partner?

The way you view dating, and how you see it fitting in
your total life, will determine how the various levels of
relationship—the personal, the emotional, the physical—will fit together in *your* experience.

So you ought to make your basic decisions now. You
ought to decide now how the physical is going to fit into
your dating life. Why decide *now*? Mainly because the
time to make this kind of decision isn't when you're being
jolted by those surging love feelings we've talked
about. The time is when you're outside the situation, able
to consider all sides of the issue. Not that the Holy Spirit
can't lead you *then*. It's just that you're more likely to look
to Him for guidance now!

But what's involved in making decisions now? Basically
it's balancing the personal, emotional and physical aspects of dating. Deciding ahead of time how they fit together. You can take a shot now, using the dating guide
chart on page 88. Fit in opposite each "contact level" the
level from each progression list adjacent that seems to fit.

For instance, you may decide that the first few dates are
basis only for telling that a guy or gal seems nice and is
fun. If so (even if love feelings start bubbling up inside),
you may think that all the affection level warrants is "like
better than most others." Those love feelings may not be
for the person; you may just be falling in love with love.

What fits in on the physical level? You decide.

Using the chart will help you face some pretty important issues. How deeply should you go on the personal
and affection levels before you'll want to go steady? What
fits physically there? Again, you decide.

Here are lists of progression. Why not try it now?

You may not want to leave your chart the way you've
filled it out today. It probably would be helpful to come
back and think this through more carefully another time.

Progression lists

personal level	affectional level	physical level
looks, seems nice	enjoy being with him/her	hold hands
pleasant, good sense of humor, fun to be with	like better than most others	kiss cuddle
we have similar interests, likes and dislikes	like better than any of several	neck light petting
we feel free to talk honestly about ourselves	experience love feelings for him/her	heavy petting (under clothing)
we talk about, share spiritual experiences	both like as a person and love	heavy petting (without clothing)
we have the same attitudes toward basic issues of life	respect; willing to commit self to him/her for life actually do commit self, totally and finally	intercourse

But until you do, why not use the chart as a dating guide? Let it mark the restrictions you yourself set for casual dating. And—stay inside your own limits.

Steps to take

1. Evaluate: "Pick only a date who would make a good mate." Do you agree or disagree? Why?

2. Commit. Use the chart on page 88 to decide how you'll set your own dating plans and limits.

Figure 1

DATING GUIDE CHART

Contact Level	Personal Level	Emotional Level	Physical Level
First few dates			
Several dates			
Steady dating			
Engagement			
Marriage			

8

To pet, or not to pet

To pet or not to pet. That *is* a question!

It's interesting to look through Christian books about sex written to college kids. They all seem to agree that the best answer is *not*. Why? Well, here are some typical reasons.

Once too much intimacy has been allowed, it becomes more difficult for the two to get to know one another personally. The impelling desire for a deeper experience and more intimate touch dominates the mind. Each time they meet they want to start where they left off before; their growing knowledge of each other becomes stunted.[1]

An Inter-Varsity booklet declares:

"Petting" in campus vocabulary is the exploitation of physical stimuli for the purpose of erotic pleasure. There is a legitimate place for pleasurable physical contact as a necessary part of preliminary love play; the objection to "petting" is that it involves the deliberate pursuit of sexual excitation, even to the point of orgasm, apart from and independently of the final act of intercourse. Christians believe that physical intercourse is properly reserved for the married state. The objection to petting is that it deliberately initiates a sequence of events in separation from their natural end.[2]

William Hulme, Lutheran theologian and experienced counselor, views petting as activity "with sexual pleasure as its purpose." He says, "The indulgence in sexual excitation for its own sake causes sex to lose its personal significance. Like a drug it demands heavier dosages to satisfy its desires."[3]

To the argument that petting is an expression of love, Hulme replies:

> This rationale fails to reckon with the nature of eros love. As they involve themselves in sex-play, the couple's desire for sexual union simply increases. When petting is with the same person, eros becomes increasingly demanding. The couple may seek to meet these demands with more intense and intimate sex-play. As they stop short of intercourse at these intense expressions of petting, the frustration can be greater—and more "unnatural"—than in less intimate expressions of affection.[4]
>
> The difficulty in trying to justify petting to a climax as an alternative to sexual intercourse is that there is only a hair splitting difference. The advantage is that it is safe so far as avoiding pregnancy is concerned. Otherwise the problem is similar to that of premarital intercourse. The intimate expression of the marital commitment is experienced without the commitment. In a sense this is a form of cheating. In premarital intercourse the sign of one-flesh is expressed without the *relationship* of one-flesh. In petting to a climax the *pleasure* of the sign is experienced apart from the sign.[5]

Hulme concludes his evaluation of petting by focusing on the impact of sexual love on relationship. If you resist petting (or back up after having gone too far), "you preserve sex from becoming an end in itself in your courtship" and preserve its meaningfulness for marriage. By giving the relationship priority, you keep sex from becoming an end in itself, and from becoming a destructive force in your life.[6]

A destructive force?

Looking back through these quotes we can pick out ideas suggested in earlier chapters. Like the idea that sex is related primarily to commitment, and secondarily to love. In the context of full commitment (marriage), full physical expression of love feelings is not only right and enjoyable, it's important. Apart from full commitment, sex play becomes an end, a seeking of pleasure or security or reassurance that the other person really cares for us. These writers believe sexual activity out of context is outside the framework of God's purpose and a twisting of the potential He planted in each of our personalities.

Looking back you can see, too, an echo of the idea that what is most important in building a realtionship is development of the personal level of acquaintance. Not the physical level.

And then, there's the idea that petting and other intimate forms of sex play are destructive—destructive even when the two involved really believe they love each other, and have gone together for a long time.

Can we really buy this idea?

There are several ways that petting was described as destructive by the fellows and girls who contributed to this book.

A California girl says:

Too often kids misinterpret their physical attraction to someone as love. They don't know how to distinguish between physical desires and true emotions toward a person. They get physically excited after petting (or just making out) and they think it's their means of expressing

their feelings for that person. The relationship becomes
purely physical, and usually they lack spiritual or intel-
lectual communication. Kids need to know a person
through true communication before they need to affec-
tionately express themselves. A desire for physical expression often comes from insecurity—the need to feel
wanted.

"Why isn't sex a valid expression of true mature love?"
asked one girl who wrote in. The answer of course is that
sex is! But the real queston is What's "true mature love"?
It's hardly love feelings for a person you don't know very
well. And "true mature love" is hardly excitement in the
seat of a parked car.

But those love feelings can lead to trouble. At least in
the view of this Indiana eighteen-year-old:

> Most kids use "falling in love" very loosely. Three or
> four times a year *really* isn't uncommon. And of course
> love merits a little more sex activity than a more *casual*
> relationship. Maybe it starts with a prolonged good-night
> kiss. But since you went that far with the last person with
> whom you had a *casual* relationship (we've forgotten that
> we were "in love" then, too), it's only right to give more
> this time.

Remember Jim's comment in an earlier chapter? "Once
a guy has touched a girl he wants more and more. Today's
environment in high school even encourages it, makes
jokes of it, and denies anything wrong with it, 'it' being
petting. Once a Christian gets involved, if he really wants
to live for Christ, he *wants* to get out but continually goes
back. This, of course, is the boy's point of view. He wants
the pleasure again, and each time he gains it, it gains
more of a grip on him."

See the shift here? *It's away from a focus on the person,
toward a focus on the pleasure!*

Programmed body, programmed mind

"We're so tired of hearing 'save sex till marriage,' " says one fellow. "But yet, it's so important. And we don't realize how common it will seem to know your wife has kissed and petted with every boy in school—and that you really aren't special."

So a lot of kids feel they're in a bind. "It's terribly unrealistic to say that a couple are going to go together for six months, and end up with a light peck on the cheek," complains a California girl. "But on the other hand," she goes on, "how do you avoid guilt feelings?"

What she's saying is this. Nobody in our culture expects to restrain themselves in dating. But if you don't restrain yourself, you slip into patterns that make you feel guilty.

Earlier we set the outer limits. We labeled intercourse as definitely wrong, on clear scriptural grounds. In the last chapter, you set a few limits at the other extreme. Limits on how far you want to go in a casual situation, and how far in a steady relationship. You may have puzzled a bit (like a lot of other kids) about petting. Certainly it's somewhere between intercourse and holding hands. But where? And why?

Our survey up to now has made two points clear. Older Christians who have evaluated petting in light of God's purpose in sex have felt that it's out of line. You may feel differently. But a lot of kids who've been there are less than enthusiastic. You may feel that you're not like these kids. Who knows? Maybe you're not.

But then, maybe you are!

How can you find out? Before you decide, you ought to think through a couple of concepts that young people often share.

We have to learn from experience. One nineteen-year-old girl says:

> You simply can't set up personal standards for yourself till you've faced the physical and emotional needs you have. But once you realize these needs, it's entirely too easy to rationalize away everything and anything. I went with a guy for a while, had a few heavy petting sessions, and suddenly woke up to find out that I'd lost respect for him, and he for me. Afterwards we were both sorry, but how else could we learn?

Can this be right? Can't we know till it's too late? Isn't

there any way to find out about a thing except to try it and see?

A fire looks hot, and when you get close to it you can feel the warmth. Is sticking your hand right in—to try it and see—the only way to know if it will burn?

"Go slow on the next curve," a motorist warns. "It's slick ice, and you'll never make it going the speed limit." Is the only way to find out to accelerate, and see?

A school text explains gravity as the attraction between two masses, and tells you why things always fall down instead of up. Is jumping off a ten-story building the only way to be sure that you'd fall instead of floating off into the clouds? Do you have to try it to see?

The "you've got to try it" philosophy sounds pretty silly in these cases. Far more silly than it sounds when it's applied to petting. For one thing, you can believe there might be exceptions to the "petting leads to frustration, guilt, and distrust" suggestion of our Indiana friend. But it's hard to find exceptions to the ideas that fire burns, that an ice-slick highway isn't safe, and that when you fall it's always down, not up.

But the issue isn't whether or not you can find exceptions. The issue is *What kind of evidence permits us to know ahead of time whether something is safe or dangerous?*

We can feel the warmth of the fire before we feel its searing heat, and we accept this as evidence. We hear the testimony of a man who's been on the icy highway, and we accept his word as evidence. We understand how gravity works, and we accept this explanation as evidence. In each case, we accept *evidence* in place of direct experience. And we're pretty sure that we "know."

Well, then, what about petting? Do we have any evidence?

Our feelings provide one line of evidence. Visualize

yourself in a petting situation. Then picture yourself coming home and describing exactly what happened, step by step, to the Lord in prayer. Can you do it without a sense of guilt? If not, why feel you have to actually *do it* to know whether or not you'll feel guilty?

What about the evidence from guys and girls quoted in this book? They're not reported here to scare. They're quoted because when kids were asked to share their experiences and questions with you, this is what they wrote. And *not one Christian kid of the three thousand involved came out and said, "Tell the kids to pet; it's great."* Everyone who shared an experience talked about the problems petting caused. So I really haven't loaded the quotes. This is what they really said.

With testimony like this from the ones who've been there, do you really think a person has to try it out to know if it might be harmful?

Then there's the evidence from "how it works." When you ask what the purpose of petting is *biologically*, it's pretty clear that petting is part of a pattern of sexual stimulation leading naturally to intercourse. "The various forms of petting are," says another Inter-Varsity publication, "the natural prelude to the intimacies of marriage. Failure to realize this physiological purpose can lead to some serious consequences."[7]

Biologically petting isn't designed to *satisfy* our emotions, but to *stimulate* and *excite* us, and lead to the fullest expression of sex in marriage.

So don't shrug off the idea that maybe you ought to make some decisions *before* you get into a situation and learn from experience. You can't honestly say, "There's no other way for me to know."

"I can't help it." This is another popular idea. "I didn't mean to do what I did. But out there alone, well, we just lost control. We just couldn't help it."

Sometimes this is true. Once a guy is really aroused, he may lose control. Once a girl is turned on, she may lose control too. Not that she gets aggressive. Just the opposite for most. An aroused girl often feels languid, relaxed, receptive. In this situation she may not be able to say "Stop" either.

So what's to do? Pass it all off with an "I guess it's natural, then"?

When a drunk smashes into a car full of teenagers (as recently happened here in Phoenix where I'm writing this), he can't help it either. Under the influence of liquor he simply *can't* drive safely. But do we pass this off with an "Oh well. Better luck next time"? Hardly! We feel that the drunk was responsible. No, not responsible for what he couldn't do. *But responsible to stop when he could!*

It's the same way with sex. Maybe when we're really under the influence of our sex drive we can't stop. But we sure are responsible to stop before we're that far gone!

Where's the stopping point? For some who drink, the stopping point is the first glass. Once they take the first one, they can't stop. If you've already programmed your body and mind with an overdose of sexual stimulation, the chances are the stopping point for you may well be Christie's "simple kiss."

Somewhere in this pattern there is a place where you ought to stop. When you can "help it."

Who is responsible to call the halt? The usual suggestion is that it's the girl's responsibility, because she's aroused later than the guy. But that's not a very good argument. Why? Because everyone is responsible for himself, and for others. "Look after each other," says the Bible, "so that not one of you will fail to find God's best blessings" (Heb. 12:15). And the Bible also says, "Don't you realize that you can choose your own master? [See? The choice *isn't* your date's, it's *yours*!] You can choose sin (with death) or else obedience (with acquittal). The one to whom you offer yourself, he will take you and be your master and you will be his slave" (Rom. 6:16).

Figure 2
Progression of sexual feelings

being together ——▶ hand holding ——▶ good night kiss
(no sexual feelings aroused)

prolonged kiss—▶ necking ——▶ petting—▶ heavy petting
(male sexual feelings aroused)   (female sexual feelings aroused)

mutual sex play ——▶ sexual intercourse

You may plead later, "I couldn't help it." But you can never hide from yourself the knowledge that somewhere along the line you did choose.

Too late?
An eighteen-year-old Minnesota boy says:

I abhor the stereotyped image of a Christian fellow or his girl as a person who is ashamed of and a little scared of sex. And I equally abhor the over-reaction to this neurotic, Puritan view that Christians sometimes manifest with a smart-aleck, "snicker" attitude. Christian teens should be open, clean, and unafraid of sex, conscious that it's a gift from God. They shouldn't equate the body with evil, but must realize that God approves of sex rightly used.

It's a good portrait. A Christian *shouldn't* be ashamed or afraid of sex. He should be open, unafraid, because he recognizes God's lordship over this part of his life, and frankly adopts standards that will please Him.

But what about the guy or girl who already has gone too far? What about the kids with the programmed bodies

and minds, who feel guilt and frustration and have lost
respect for themselves and their dates?

It's late for the kids who yelled, "Help!" But it's not too
late.

That's one thing about being a Christian. Sure, when
we sin we suffer. When we do what we believe is wrong,
we feel guilty. We *are* guilty.

But the Christian has forgiveness for the asking, and a
chance to start over again, cleansed.

There's no promise that it will be easy. It'll be hard. But
there is the promise of a way. The Bible says that by His
mighty power God "has given us . . . rich and wonderful
blessings . . . ; for instance, the promise to save us from
the lust and rottenness all around us, and to give us his
own character. But to obtain these gifts, you need more
than faith; you must also work hard to be good, and even
that is not enough. For then you must learn to know God
better and discover what He wants you to do. Next, learn
to put aside your own desires so that you will become
patient and godly, gladly letting God have His way. This
will make possible the next step, which is for you to enjoy
other people and to like them, and finally you will grow to
love them deeply. The more you go on in this way, the
more you will grow strong spiritually and become fruitful
and useful to our Lord Jesus Christ" (2 Peter 1:4-8).

Steps to take

1. What does the author mean by the phrase "pro-
    grammed mind and programmed body"? Relate
    this idea to the common concept that "we've got
    to try it to know."

2. Look over the chart on progression of sexual feel-
    ings (p. 98), and decide now just how far you

intend to go. Where is your stop?

If necessary, revise the chart you worked on in this last chapter (p. 88).

3. If you've already gone "too far," read 1 John 1:9 and study carefully 2 Peter 1:4-8 at the end of this chapter. What steps do you need to take for re-commitment.

9

The real thing

"What," asks a California college freshman, "is the difference between infatuation, desire, love and trust?"

It's hard to understand, much less explain. But it sure is important. Especially with teens who feel they're in love and considering marriage. Apparently many with good intentions and enough confidence to take that step of complete commitment have been wrong. For one of two teenage marriages ends in separation or divorce! Even for those who stay together, "there is no question that a tragically high percentage of the young married couples who remain married are disillusioned and dissatisfied with their marriage to the point where it has become a bore, a mockery, a burden, a failure."[1]

How do kids expect to tell when they're really in love? Here are the tests suggested by kids in one Illinois high school. You'll note that their ideas range from the wildly romantic to the rather mature.

A couple, they said, really knows they are in love when:

neither likes to be away from the other

they want to share everything with each other

they think about each other all the time

they enjoy the same things and agree on morals,
        religion, life, etc.

they would say anything they think to the other
        and be understood

they both feel they have a complete understanding
        of each other and are able to accept the
        other as they really are

they want the very best for each other and put the
        other person ahead of themselves

they respect each other enough to wait until
        they're married because they don't want to
        hurt each other

they would both be willing, at times, to sacrifice
        their own comforts for the comfort of each
        other

Some of these are pretty good tests. But all are hard to
apply. For instance, take the idea that if you're really in
love you "have a complete understanding of each other
and are able to accept each other as they really are." It
sounds great. The trouble is, it just can't happen. You
don't get a "complete understanding" of the other in
dating, or even in engagement. It's not until you live together, till you face the little irritations and the bigger
conflicts, that you find out what each of you is really like.
Under this pressure, dating's "complete understandings"
have a way of disappearing. Or else understanding
grows, and over a period of time you do come to accept
and fully love each other.

But that's part of marriage. It doesn't come before. And
it's dangerous to confuse this truth with the early glow of

love feelings that make us gloss over faults and touch up the one we love with virtues we only imagine he or she has. The fact is, *no one* is as perfect as we think the one we love is. And when we find that out, we have a jolt coming.

What makes us think we really love someone when we don't? One author suggested several love counterfeits, motives for love that are less than the real thing.[2]

Under pressure

Most guys and girls have needs, pressures within their own personalities, that can push them into an unreal love. These needs make certain counterfeits especially attractive to them. What are some of the things commonly misunderstood as real love?

This "success forecast for young marriages"[3] shows some factors besides love that ought to be considered in making the big decision.

Love as fun. There's nothing wrong in wanting to have fun. Or in dating kids with whom you have a good time. Obviously, dates ought to have fun together.

But if you're the fun-loving type who slips away from duller responsibilities, and the big thing that attracts you to your guy or gal is the fun you have on a date, back off. There's no proof that it's love.

There's lots more to life than the fun times we have on dates. Being married cuts down on freedom and relaxation, and forces us all to dig in and work. "Love" that looks at life together as one big blast is way, way out.

Love as glamour. He's the football hero; she's the beauty queen. What a perfect match! Each right at the top of campus society.

Trouble is, if you're a guy or girl who is deeply concerned about campus prestige, you may confuse the *status* of your date with qualities that make for a solid marriage. You may love not because of *who* he is, but because of *what* he is.

Love as shared misery. You're unhappy at home, misunderstood and mistreated. Then you find that gal or guy who's in the same fix—who understands. It's not hard to convince yourself that this is love. *If we were only married,* you think, *we'd have a different homelife. Then our problems would be over.*

Getting married to dodge one set of troubles, though, usually means jumping right into others you're not prepared for. And shared misery isn't a good foundation for the real thing.

Love as rebellion. Everyone needs to be on his own. For high schoolers and collegians this is a dominating need.

You've got to find and be yourself.

So if parents try to dominate you, try to direct everything in your life, you're probably going to rebel. You may not rebel consciously. But down deep there's a need to strike out on your own, to prove yourself. Sometimes this too is confused with love. You're driven into the relationship by your parent's opposition. The more they criticize and disapprove, the more you're sure that this is *the* one.

Love as sexual attraction. We've talked a lot about this already. But it's worth saying again. When the physical becomes dominant in a relationship, you're in for trouble.

That's why petting, even for steadies and engaged couples, can hurt rather than help. The focus shifts from the person to the body, from concern for the other to the exciting sensations and emotions *I* feel. Sexual attraction may seem to hold you together, but in the long run you begin to lose respect for the other and for yourself.

Maybe you've wondered, as the rather black picture of petting was sketched last chapter by various writers and the kids themselves, why sex in marriage isn't a perverted thing too. Why doesn't the experience of married sex drive you to think about sex all the time? Or to think of your husband or wife as a thing to use rather than as a person?

Let's admit first that sex in marriage *can* be perverted. Just because a minister has said holy words over you, and just because you've made open promises to love and to honor, doesn't mean you'll have married sex in perspective. Some men and women go through marriage after marriage, looking for something satisfying in their relationship. But because they look for it in sex as sex, they never find it.

Sex for sex's sake can motivate in marriage as well as

outside. That's why the Bible says "Don't marry in lust, as the pagans do." When you marry, make it for something more.

But, again, how can petting and other intimate sex play in marriage not warp us as they seem to outside marriage?

For one thing, in marriage petting and sex play can take their correct biological and emotional role, as preparation for intercourse. In marriage "all the way" is *the* way, and sex play prepares you both for fullest satisfaction. Outside of marriage sex play is an end. It's indulged in to satisfy—but it can only stimulate. And thus outside of marriage it's frustrating—frustrating to the point that sex can dominate our thoughts or our relationships. When sex is satisfying, then it can be enjoyed and take its natural (not dominating) place in our lives.

For another thing, sex outside of marriage quickly comes to dominate a relationship? Why? Because you and the other person live divided lives, *except romantically*. The humdrum and routine are lived at home with others. The only life you share with your date is sexual.

When you marry you have to share everything. The wet stockings in the bathroom, the dishes that have to be washed, the bills that have to be paid, the little frustrations and the daily decisions that make much of everyone's life seem routine. When you live together totally—sharing the humdrum of life as well as the magic—sex seems to fit more easily. It's a part of your life together, but certainly not the whole thing.

So if your "true love" is based only on sexual compatibility, watch out. Life together *isn't*.

On faith

In a very real sense everyone marries on faith. You *can't* know that what you feel is the real thing. The real thing is something that comes by growth—by growth when two lives are lived together for a long time. Only when you've lived together can you know.

All our ideas about love have some truth in them. Yet all are incomplete. Shouldn't we be drawn sexually to someone we love? Certainly. And in a vitally alive and growing marriage this joy is never old or routine or distasteful. Yet sexual attraction *alone* is never strong enough to produce a steadfast love. It takes harmony on every level to nurture sexual love. The couples who fight over money, who nag each other, who make cutting remarks that hurt and belittle, will hardly have a satisfactory sex life. Sexual attraction crumbles under the pressure of living together without a deep, Godlike loyalty undergirding your love.

Should marriage meet your needs? Certainly. This was basic in God's original plan. But love is no substitute to facing up to our problems. It's no escape from ourselves. To some extent we have to be mature enough to handle the pressures we're under *before* marriage to sucessfully tackle the pressures of marriage. It may seem hard to believe, but it's true. The pressures and problems in marriage are bigger than whatever problems you're facing just now.

So all our love feelings, all our attraction to that guy or gal, are no sure foundation for marriage. They're no way to tell if it's the real thing. Marriage is a step each of us must take on faith.

Are there ways to test the reality of our love? Yes, some.

We can wait. Let our relationship grow before we marry, instead of rushing into marriage as though afraid we might fall out of love if we don't hurry.

We can separate. Not permanently, of course. But instead of spending *all* our time with each other, we can do things with other guys or girls. We can develop hobbies, work on school or church projects, study, learn, grow. We can keep all of life in perspective, instead of investing all our time and all our thoughts in each other. Life is too big to be summed up in two people, too big to have its only meaning in young love.

We can exercise self-control. Too much physical intimacy can throw any relationship off track. We can lose ourselves too easily in the exciting sensations aroused. And we can begin to believe that, because we excite each other, we're made for each other. But love is too big to be summed up in sex. And self-control won't hurt us.

And, we can take the humdrum test. We can plan *not* to make all our dates moonlight and roses. We can see each other when we don't look and feel romantic. Sitting around the house together, studying, doing dishes, talking—with a hands-off policy in force—can help us find out if we really bore each other except when sex is central in the relationship.

Tests like these will help. But they still aren't an answer. When you marry, it's still got to be on faith. You can't *know*.

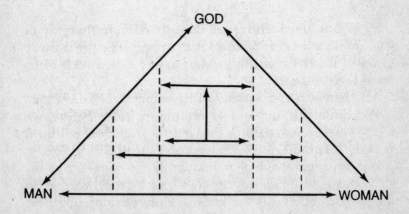

That's why an eighteen-year-old Michigan teen's advice (and this little diagram he enclosed) is so important: "Many Christians don't understand the principle of dating—that two only really grow together when they grow together in God. As the two grow close to God, they grow closer to each other."

Knowing whom to marry isn't just looking at our feelings, or at the other's qualities. It's important to look to God. You can't know, but He can. And He does.

Nothing in a Christian's life is to be done apart from God. It's all part of our walk by faith. We know that God is a Person. We know He loves us, and is ready and willing to guide us through life. So ultimately all the tests of love give way to one question: Are you sure it's God's will for you to marry this person? Have you talked to Him about it? Do you have a sense of peace and assurance inside?

"You will be judged," says the Bible, "on whether or not you are doing what Christ wants you to do" (James 2:12). Not on whether you kept inside the confines of our little lists of dos and don'ts. But on one issue: Were you responsive to Christ? Did you do what He wanted you to do?

One of the first ways to make sure that your choice is His choice is to bring God into your dating. Bring Him into casual relationships, and especially into your steady relationships.

Pray about your dating. Pray with your date. Talk together about the Lord and share your experiences with Him. All this will help you grow closer to God, and, if this *is* God's choice for you, closer to your girl friend or boyfriend.

Whatever you do together that cuts you off from God cuts you off from really knowing each other. It's only as you grow together in God that you'll be able to grow, really, together.

By faith

God is bound to have an impact on your dating, one way or another. And He's got the solution to the problems and questions you have with sex. We'll see how in the next chapter.

But for now, while we consider the "real thing," it's enough to remember that everybody has to choose a partner on faith. But the Christian has a chance to choose *by* faith.

That's too great a chance to throw away!

10

The answer

Linda, a Texas girl who helped with this book, tells a story about temptation running riot. Here it is, just as she wrote it out:

A girl I know had a serious problem with her thought life (in the sexual realm). Before becoming a Christian, she had engaged in some rather immoral practices (not, however, to the point of having intercourse with a man); and her reading of novels heavily sprinkled with risque incidents, coupled with her attendance at movies of the same sort, had filled her mind with all sorts of ideas. She actually used to be eager to get to bed at night so that she could begin rehearsing in her mind the latest sexual dramas which she had dreamed up. Naturally, after she was saved, she was convicted of the wrongness of these practices; but the thoughts were still in her head, and the stimuli still lay all around her.

She has found that the solution is twofold:

(1) She must avoid reading books and watching TV shows and movies which supply source material for immoral thoughts—must also stop thinking of past personal incidents.

(2) She must *overtly surrender* her thoughts to the
Lord, returning again to Philippians 4:8 for cor-
rection and encouragement. By training her
mind to dwell on the items characterized by the
adjectives in this verse, she has been able to
change her thought pattern significantly.

The whole process of "cleaning up her mind" has ex-
tended over some three years; but her progress has been
amazing. She no longer needs to be as careful about slight
stimuli—of course, temptations still come continually, but
she claims 1 Corinthians 10:13 and rereads Philippians 4:8
and applies it. By the time she's gone halfway through that
verse, dwelling on illustrations of each word which she
has seen in her own experience, the temptation has usually been successfully met, and her thoughts have been
turned in a positive direction.

Real victory over a very real problem; a problem experienced by *so* many kids.

Her story concludes with these words: "It's true, 'cause
I'm the girl."

Becoming a Christian

When you read through Linda's story, several phrases
point the way to the answer, to "real victory."

The first is just this: "Becoming a Christian."

Why is becoming a Christian so important? Can't
non-Christians be moral people? Sure. Many of them are.
But there's more to the Christian faith than simple morality. Two big things are particularly important for all of us.

We step into relationship with Jesus Christ. The Apostle
Paul was a religious man before he became a Christian.
He was a highly moral man, who zealously tried to obey
God's laws. "But," he wrote, looking back, "whatever
gain I had, I counted as loss for the sake of Christ. Indeed I
count everything as loss because of the surpassing worth
of knowing Christ Jesus my Lord" (Phil. 3:7-8 RSV).

His *religion* was replaced by a *relationship*.

It was to make this possible for all of us that Christ died. Remember what "flesh" indicates in most New Testament passages? The fact that man comes into and lives in this world estranged—separated, cut-off—from God. This isn't God's doing. It's man's. All of us are out of step with God; He's not out of step with us. The old familiar "all have sinned" is saying just this. All of us choose to go our own way, and to turn away from God's. Something is wrong down inside us that keeps us from harmony—from relationship—with God. Because God isn't warped. He's straight. And you can't lay a crooked stick on a straight line and have them match up.

None of us has to go very far to prove to himself that sin is real in his life, that there's something there that pulls him his own way. The Bible gives us a simple test. "When someone wants to do wrong it is never God who is tempting him, for God never wants to do wrong and never tempts anyone else to do it" (James 1:13). Never wants to do wrong! Have you ever *wanted* to do something you knew was wrong? That desire didn't come from God. "Temptation is the pull of man's own evil thoughts and wishes" (James 1:14).

So something is wrong. Not just on the surface of our life, on the action level, but wrong down deep inside. We've been warped out of harmony with God, and out of relationship with Him.

That's why religion is no good. Oh, it can help us reform the outside. But it can't take out the kinks inside. It can help us be moral, but it can't bring us into harmony with God. That's something Jesus had to do for us. "When we were utterly helpless . . . , Christ came at just the right time and died for us sinners" (Rom. 5:6). The fantastic thing the Bible tells us is that somehow His death reconciled us to God (see Rom. 5:10). What does reconcile mean? To bring into harmony. To bring into relationship. Christ died, that He might bring us to God.

No wonder Paul was so enthusiastic. With religion, he'd struggled and tried without the success to reach God. But Christ stepped into our world and brought God to us! And He forgave us, reconciling us to God by His death.

So that's one thing that becoming a Christian can mean to us. Suddenly—we know God.

We're changed inside. That's another thing. "You have a new life. It was not passed on to you from your parents, for the life they gave you will fade away. This new one will last forever, for it comes from Christ, God's everliving Message to men" (1 Peter 1:23).

The Bible talks about this new life in many ways. It's called becoming "alive" (Col. 3:1), being "born into God's family" (1 John 3:9), being given a "new nature" (Eph. 4:24). All these are ways of saying that a new and vital force is planted in our personalities when we come to know Christ. It's a force that *wants* to do right, that is contrary to the force of sin that pulls us toward wrong. More important, unlike conscience, this new life provides a motivation that can actually help us change. No, not one that will change automatically. But now there's a basis for victory. Now we *can* live for Christ if we so choose.

"If you have really heard His voice and learned from Him the truths concerning Himself [relationship], then throw off your old evil nature—the old you that was a partner in your evil ways—rotten through and through, full of lust and sham. Now your attitudes and thoughts must all be constantly changing for the better; yes, you must *be* a new and different person, holy and good. Clothe yourself with this new nature" (Eph. 4:21-24).

So becoming a Christian is the first step toward overcoming *any* temptation. And it certainly is the first step toward living with sex in perspective and under control.

It was the first step for our Texas girl, Linda. And it's the first step for you.

Cleaning up the mind

Receiving a new life from God and stepping into a personal relationship with Jesus Christ is the key to victory—but not the victory itself. Girls and guys who become Christians, or who have grown up as Christians, still get in spots where they have to yell, "Help!"

Gene, who was a Christian teen, still cried out, "I think these thoughts all the time. Nothing seems to help. What can I do?" The "new" inside Gene cried out for freedom. But he felt trapped. The "old" was inside too, and the "old" was firmly in control. The Bible's command "Get rid of all that is wrong in your life, both inside and outside, and be humbly glad for the wonderful message we have received" (James 1:21) *sounds* great. But it's not easy.

That's why we have a promise—and a part. God has brought us the victory way. He's given us the resources. It's up to us to use them. "Remember," the James passage goes on, "it is a message to obey, not just to listen to. So don't fool yourselves" (v. 22).

What are we to do?

Well take a look at Linda's solution. She had a mind filled with "sexual dramas."

"As a man thinks in his heart, so he is" is a familiar proverb. But we don't realize how dynamically true this is. You *do* become what you feed your mind.

If you feed your mind on sex tales, and avidly reread erotic descriptions of all sorts of sex acts, it's going to affect you. If you keep your eyes fastened on *Playboy's* center section and other assorted nudes, it's going to affect you. If you take in the movies that are produced to excite and stimulate, it's going to affect you.

That's the background of a peculiar principle you find in the Bible. "A person who is pure of heart," it says, "sees goodness and purity in everything; but a person whose own heart is evil and untrusting finds evil in everything, for his dirty mind and rebellious heart color all he sees and hears" (Titus 1:15).

Recall one of Linda's comments. The thoughts were still in her head after conversion, "and the stimuli still lay all around." Well, she's right. Stimuli do lie all around. The clothes the fellows and girls wear, the way they carry themselves, advertising in the newspapers and magazines, the books, TV, the movies, the talk on campus. The stimuli are all around. And *if your mind is keyed to sex*, it will pick up the stimuli and focus your thoughts right where you don't want them to be! A "dirty mind" colors all we see and hear.

So Linda took exactly the right step in seeking her solution.

She *avoided the source material for immoral thoughts*, and she *overtly surrendered her thoughts to the Lord*.

"Run from anything that gives you the evil thoughts that young men often have" the Bible says, "but stay close to anything that makes you want to do right" (2 Tim. 2:22*a*.). The way to overcome temptations that come to us through the mind is to avoid source material for evil thoughts. Don't think you can enjoy smutty paperbacks from the corner drugstore and keep spiritually healthy and strong. You become what you feed your mind.

Paul says it again in Philippians 4:8, the verse that Linda found so helpful: "Fix your thoughts on what is true and good and right. Think about things that are pure and lovely, and on the fine, good things in others. Think about all you can praise God for and be glad about." Paul continues: "Keep putting into practice all you learned from me and saw me doing, and the God of peace will be with you" (v. 9).

That's the great thing about cleaning up the mind as a Christian. It's not a do-it-yourself project. The God of peace will be with you.

"No amount of chiding," adds an Indiana fellow we've heard from before, "will make a noticeable contribution to moral improvement. The power must come from the Holy Spirit." Because Christians are in relationship with Christ, that power is ours. He's entered our lives—your life—to live with you, and to make it possible for you to be free of all bondage. "Your old evil desires were nailed to the cross with Him; that part of you that loves to sin was crushed and fatally wounded, so that your sin-loving body is no longer under sin's control, no longer needs to be a slave to sin" (Rom. 6:6). With Christ, with a new life from Him, we *can* be free. "Do not let sin control your . . . body any longer; do not obey it; do not give in to its sinful desires" (v. 12).

And you begin to take back control by cleaning up your mind.

Setting limits

A sixteen-year-old girl from Pennsylvania says:

> Lots of kids have constantly been fed the idea that sex is a very strong instinct. They may even nod their heads and agree. But they allow themselves to get into situations they think they can handle, and generally don't realize the pull sex has. It's not that they want to prove by experience. It's just that the idea applies to "someone else." We don't like to hear "You're seeing too much of him. Your emotions can't take it." We tend to trust our own impulses.

But you can't trust your own impulses. None of us can.

That's why in this book you've been asked to set limits for yourself—now.

Set limits that fit in with God's ideas on sex, not some paperback's. And not even teen society's. Oh, I know. You might get the feeling that you're just not with it. That your world is spinning away from you, playing it fast and a little loose, and that you're missing out on a lot of fun and good times. But Paul puts it pretty straight in the Bible: "Let me say this, then, speaking for the Lord: live no longer as the unsaved do, for they are blinded and confused. Their closed hearts are full of darkness; they are far away from the life of God because they have shut their minds against Him, and they cannot understand His ways" (Eph. 4:17-18).

When the pattern of life—even of dating life—in the teenage world is out of God's pattern, then you have to choose. You have to shut your mind against the world's way or against God's.

Everybody knows that you have to fit into your campus world. You have to live there. You want to be a part, and you *ought* to be a part. But where God's way of life and your world's way of life run counter to each other, then you have to choose. As I've suggested in another book,[1] you don't have to *conform* to fit into your world. And the Bible makes it clear that you can't conform to the world and still be a friend of God. You are to be living a brand-new kind of life that is always learning more and more what is right, and trying to be more and more like Christ, who created this new life within you (see Col. 1:10).

Sometimes we're just afraid to go God's way. Afraid of what it might cost us. Of what we might miss. But "we need have no fear of someone who loves us perfectly; his

perfect love for us elimi-
nates all dread of what
he might do to us. If we
are afraid, it is for fear of
what he might do to us,
and shows that we are not
fully convinced that he
really loves us" (1 John
4:18).

Are you sure God loves
you? Then why be afraid of His way? Why be afraid of
limitations you feel He wants you to set? Whatever God
wants for us, He wants because He loves us "perfectly,"
not with a warped love that uses us, or enjoys seeing us
suffer. Perfect love wants the very best for us.

So if you limit yourself to doing what God wants, you needn't do it from a sense of duty. You can do it with joy, realizing that His way is the way of love. The way to find His very best for you.

And it is important to live this way, staying within His limits and being responsive to His will. Even when it's hard.

It's the way to maturity. "Is your life full of difficulties and temptations?" the Apostle James asks. "Then be happy, for when the way is rough, your patience has a chance to grow. So let it grow, and don't try to squirm out of your problems. For when your patience is finally in full bloom, then you will be ready for anything, strong in character, full and complete" (James 1:2-4).

An infant lives on impulse. He crys and grasps and has to have—now. But maturity is marked by self-control. By checking your impulses that you might reach greater, self-chosen goals. The baby's body dominates his life. The body doesn't dominate mature men or women. They see more to life than food and drink and warmth—and sex.

Responding to God, setting the limits He shows you, doing what He wants you to do, is the only way to gain strength of character—to become the mature person you really want to be.

It's the way to spiritual reality. "You will never be able," the Bible warns, "to eat solid spiritual food and understand the deeper things of God's Word until you become better Christians and learn right from wrong *by practicing doing right*" (Heb. 5:14).

Stepping out of God's will, refusing to do what He wants you to do, stunts your spiritual growth. It cuts you out of a close, person-to-person fellowship with Christ.

This fellowship is terribly important. As we said,

Christianity isn't a religion. It's a relationship. A relationship with Jesus Christ, who is eager to live life with the person who trusts Him. Eager to take the uncertainty, the guilt, the fear away. Eager to provide the power needed to make us the vibrant, mature individuals we yearn to be.

Apart from this relationship, Christianity has nothing special to offer. Apart from Christ it breaks down to religion—to rules, to routine, to struggling alone on our own resources. But with Christ, God Himself enters our life and transfuses all of His vitality. All of His strength. All of His wisdom. And life has a new dimension, a new meaning, a new perspective.

"How can we be sure that we belong to Him?" asks 1 John 2:3*a*. "By looking within ourselves: are we really trying to do what He wants us to?" (v. 3*b*). Apart from obedience, from *responding to Christ*, life drifts back to routine. Back to uncertainty. Back to groping.

You may be a Christian. But it takes a *growing* relationship with Christ to make your experience match up with your resources. Setting limits, doing what's right, living responsively with Him, is the only way to reality.

It's the way to meaning. "I live in eager expectation and hope that I will never do anything that will cause me to be ashamed of myself," wrote the Apostle Paul from prison, "but that I will always be ready to speak out boldly for Christ . . . and that I will always be an honor to Christ, whether I live or whether I must die" (Phil. 1:20).

Recall the guy who commented about sex, "That's what we're for, isn't it?" He was wrong. Life is just too big and too important to be summed up in the coupling of two bodies. We're *not* here for sex. We're here for Christ. And putting anything besides Christ in the center of our lives leads to tragedy.

Each of us has to decide what life *is* for. If life is for sex, live for it. Live for the excitement, for the exhilaration of each fresh conquest. But if you do, you'll never experience the depths of sexuality, depths that are reserved for just two who commit themselves to each other for life. If you do live for sex, you'll find that as your thoughts of sex become ever more compelling and your desire more demanding, satisfaction eludes you. Because man *wasn't* made for sex. And no one finds life's meaning there.

"Your bodies were made for the Lord," the Bible says, "and He wants to fill them with Himself." Putting Christ first, filling your life with Him, doesn't mean giving up anything. It doesn't mean giving up sex. Instead it means putting sex, and everything else in life, in perspective. Putting Christ first is God's way of giving meaning to *all* life. Yes, even real meaning to that part of life which was created for sex.

Right now, for you, this means choosing.

Choosing what you'll live for. Where you'll look for meaning.

Meaning is there, in Christ. And only when you put Him there, in the center, and live life His way, will you find the meaning of sex.

Notes

Chapter 1

[1]All quotes in this book are authentic, contributed by high school and college youth from across this entire country and Canada.

Chapter 2

[1]*Premarital Sexual Standards* (pamphlet) (Washington, D.C.: Sex Information & Education Council of the U.S., 1967), p. 5.
[2]*Ibid.*, p. 7.
[3]Eugene Nida, *Customs and Cultures* (New York: Harper and Row, 1954), p. 98.

Chapter 3

[1]Quoted in Eugene Nida, *Customs and Cultures* (*op. cit.*), p. 99.
[2]Paul Ramsey, *Basic Christian Ethics* (New York: Scribner, 1950), p. 328.
[3]Ralph Eckert, "The Dating Bit—and Sex," in *Teen Love, Teen Marriage*, ed. Jules Saltman (New York: Grosset & Dunlap, 1966), p. 46.

Chapter 4

[1]*Premarital Sexual Standards* (*op. cit.*), p. 11.
[2]Gordon Smedsrud, *What Youth Are Thinking* (Minneapolis: Augsburg, 1960).

Chapter 5

[1]S. L. Halleck, quoted in news article by Ray Cromley in Ann Arbor, Mich., *Evening News.*

[2]Theodore Isaac Rubin, "A Psychiatrist's Notebook," in *Ladies' Home Journal* (Aug., 1968).

Chapter 8

[1]C. G. Scorer, *The Bible and Sex Ethics Today* (London: Inter-Varsity, 1966), p. 117.

[2]Stewart Babbage, *Christianity and Sex* (Chicago: Inter-Varsity, 1967), p. 23.

[3]William Hulme, *Youth Considers Sex* (New York: Nelson, 1965), p. 64.

[4]*Ibid.,* p. 65.

[5]*Ibid.,* p. 68.

[6]*Ibid.,* p. 72.

[7]Oliver R. Barclay, *A Time To Embrace* (pamphlet) (Chicago: Inter-Varsity, 1966), p. 19.

Chapter 9

[1]"Teen-age Marriages," in *Changing Times* (Kiplinger magazine) (Nov. 1965) p. 8.

[2]Ralph Eckert, "So You Think It's Love?" in *Teen Love, Teen Marriage* (*op. cit.*), pp. 54-60.

[3]*Changing Times, ibid.*

Chapter 10

[1]Larry Richards, *How to be Real* (Grand Rapids: Zondervan, 1979).